D0073725

Chemical Dependency

Opposing Viewpoints®

Laura K. Egendorf, *Book Editor*

Daniel Leone, *President*
Bonnie Szumski, *Publisher*
Scott Barbour, *Managing Editor*
Helen Cothran, *Senior Editor*

OPPOSING VIEWPOINTS® SERIES

Library Discard
This item has been withdrawn.

GREENHAVEN PRESS

THOMSON

GALE

362.29
C517
2003

San Diego • Detroit • New York • San Francisco • Cleveland
New Haven, Conn. • Waterville, Maine • London • Munich

© 2003 by Greenhaven Press. Greenhaven Press is an imprint of The Gale Group, Inc., a division of Thomson Learning, Inc.

Greenhaven® and Thomson Learning™ are trademarks used herein under license.

For more information, contact
Greenhaven Press
27500 Drake Rd.
Farmington Hills, MI 48331-3535
Or you can visit our Internet site at http://www.gale.com

ALL RIGHTS RESERVED.
No part of this work covered by the copyright hereon may be reproduced or used in any form or by any means—graphic, electronic, or mechanical, including photocopying, recording, taping, Web distribution or information storage retrieval systems—without the written permission of the publisher.

Every effort has been made to trace the owners of copyrighted material.

Cover credit: Planet Art

LIBRARY OF CONGRESS CATALOGING-IN-PUBLICATION DATA

Chemical dependency / Laura K. Egendorf, book editor.
    p. cm. — (Opposing viewpoints series)
Includes bibliographical references and index.
ISBN 0-7377-1221-X (pbk. : alk. paper) — ISBN 0-7377-1222-8 (lib. : alk. paper)
    1. Drug abuse—United States. 2. Drug abuse. I. Egendorf, Laura K., 1973– .
II. Series.
HV5825 .C437 2003
362.29—dc21   2002040824

Printed in the United States of America

"Congress shall make
no law...abridging the
freedom of speech, or of
the press."

First Amendment to the U.S. Constitution

The basic foundation of our democracy is the First
Amendment guarantee of freedom of expression.
The Opposing Viewpoints Series is dedicated to the
concept of this basic freedom and the idea that it is
more important to practice it than to enshrine it.

Contents

Why Consider Opposing Viewpoints?

"The only way in which a human being can make some approach to knowing the whole of a subject is by hearing what can be said about it by persons of every variety of opinion and studying all modes in which it can be looked at by every character of mind. No wise man ever acquired his wisdom in any mode but this."

John Stuart Mill

In our media-intensive culture it is not difficult to find differing opinions. Thousands of newspapers and magazines and dozens of radio and television talk shows resound with differing points of view. The difficulty lies in deciding which opinion to agree with and which "experts" seem the most credible. The more inundated we become with differing opinions and claims, the more essential it is to hone critical reading and thinking skills to evaluate these ideas. Opposing Viewpoints books address this problem directly by presenting stimulating debates that can be used to enhance and teach these skills. The varied opinions contained in each book examine many different aspects of a single issue. While examining these conveniently edited opposing views, readers can develop critical thinking skills such as the ability to compare and contrast authors' credibility, facts, argumentation styles, use of persuasive techniques, and other stylistic tools. In short, the Opposing Viewpoints Series is an ideal way to attain the higher-level thinking and reading skills so essential in a culture of diverse and contradictory opinions.

In addition to providing a tool for critical thinking, Opposing Viewpoints books challenge readers to question their own strongly held opinions and assumptions. Most people form their opinions on the basis of upbringing, peer pressure, and personal, cultural, or professional bias. By reading carefully balanced opposing views, readers must directly confront new ideas as well as the opinions of those with whom they disagree. This is not to simplistically argue that everyone who reads opposing views will—or should—change his or her opinion. Instead, the series enhances readers' understanding of their own views by encouraging confrontation with opposing ideas. Careful examination of others' views can lead to the readers' understanding of the logical inconsistencies in their own opinions, perspective on why they hold an opinion, and the consideration of the possibility that their opinion requires further evaluation.

Evaluating Other Opinions

To ensure that this type of examination occurs, Opposing Viewpoints books present all types of opinions. Prominent spokespeople on different sides of each issue as well as well-known professionals from many disciplines challenge the reader. An additional goal of the series is to provide a forum for other, less known, or even unpopular viewpoints. The opinion of an ordinary person who has had to make the decision to cut off life support from a terminally ill relative, for example, may be just as valuable and provide just as much insight as a medical ethicist's professional opinion. The editors have two additional purposes in including these less known views. One, the editors encourage readers to respect others' opinions—even when not enhanced by professional credibility. It is only by reading or listening to and objectively evaluating others' ideas that one can determine whether they are worthy of consideration. Two, the inclusion of such viewpoints encourages the important critical thinking skill of objectively evaluating an author's credentials and bias. This evaluation will illuminate an author's reasons for taking a particular stance on an issue and will aid in readers' evaluation of the author's ideas.

It is our hope that these books will give readers a deeper understanding of the issues debated and an appreciation of the complexity of even seemingly simple issues when good and honest people disagree. This awareness is particularly important in a democratic society such as ours in which people enter into public debate to determine the common good. Those with whom one disagrees should not be regarded as enemies but rather as people whose views deserve careful examination and may shed light on one's own.

Thomas Jefferson once said that "difference of opinion leads to inquiry, and inquiry to truth." Jefferson, a broadly educated man, argued that "if a nation expects to be ignorant and free . . . it expects what never was and never will be." As individuals and as a nation, it is imperative that we consider the opinions of others and examine them with skill and discernment. The Opposing Viewpoints Series is intended to help readers achieve this goal.

David L. Bender and Bruno Leone,
Founders

Greenhaven Press anthologies primarily consist of previously published material taken from a variety of sources, including periodicals, books, scholarly journals, newspapers, government documents, and position papers from private and public organizations. These original sources are often edited for length and to ensure their accessibility for a young adult audience. The anthology editors also change the original titles of these works in order to clearly present the main thesis of each viewpoint and to explicitly indicate the opinion presented in the viewpoint. These alterations are made in consideration of both the reading and comprehension levels of a young adult audience. Every effort is made to ensure that Greenhaven Press accurately reflects the original intent of the authors included in this anthology.

Introduction

"Current treatment approaches emphasize that addiction must be treated in the same way as other chronic diseases."

—*Diagnostic and Statistical Manual of Mental Disorders-IV Text Revision*

"One of the worst miscalculations of the idea that addiction and alcoholism are diseases is the notion that substance abuse can be treated away."

—*Stanton Peele*

In November 2000, California voters passed Proposition 36, known formally as the Substance Abuse and Crime Prevention Act, by a 61 to 39 percent margin. The act allows people who have been convicted of first or second time nonviolent, simple drug possession the opportunity to receive substance abuse treatment in lieu of incarceration. The proposition allocates $120 million annually for five and one half years to pay for treatment services. Studies have suggested that up to thirty-six thousand nonviolent users could be affected each year and that the initiative could save the state and local governments as much as $200 million annually due to reduced prison operation costs. Proposition 36's overwhelming victory suggests that Americans have become more accepting of the idea that drug addicts suffer from a disease that requires treatment, rather than a character fault that must be punished.

Deciding how to approach drug abuse is especially important given the increasing prevalence of drug use in the United States. According to the 2001 National Household Survey on Drug Abuse, 15.9 million Americans aged twelve or older could be classified as current illicit drug users, meaning that they had used an illegal drug at least once during the previous month. Of those substances, marijuana was the most commonly used, with 12.1 million American adolescents and adults reporting having used it during the previous month. Current users of cocaine numbered 1.7 million, while 1.3 million had taken hallucinogens and 123,000 Americans had smoked or injected heroin.

Statistics indicate that drug use is especially high among young people. For example, 10.8 percent of Americans between the ages of twelve and seventeen were current illicit drug users, compared to 9.7 percent in 2000. For young adults between the ages of eighteen and twenty-five, the increase was even sharper, rising from 15.9 percent to 18.8 percent. Overall, these two age groups were responsible for 51 percent of all illegal drug use and a disproportionate amount of inhalant and hallucinogenic abuse (76 percent and 86 percent, respectively).

However, not everyone who uses drugs becomes chemically dependent. Although the terms "substance abuse" and "chemical dependency" are often used interchangeably, there are differences between them. According to the *Diagnostic and Statistical Manual of Mental Disorders-IV Text Revision*, published by the American Psychiatric Division, "substance abuse" is associated with social factors, such as the failure to meet important obligations, multiple legal problems, drug-related arguments, and the use of drugs in dangerous situations. On the other hand, "chemical dependency" is defined by physical factors, such as increased tolerance to drugs, withdrawal symptoms, an inability to control or decrease use, and continued use despite acknowledgement of the drugs' dangerous effects.

The American view on chemical dependency has long been a dichotomy, wavering between the belief that the freedoms granted to Americans by the Constitution means that they are responsible for their behavior, and the longstanding view that addiction is a disease of the body and mind. According to William L. White, in an article for *Counselor*, "The cultural perception of opiate addiction evolved over the 19th-century from that of a misfortune, to that of a vice, to proposals that such dependence should be viewed as a disease." However, in the first half of the twentieth century, the idea that addiction was a sign of weakness reemerged. In the 1930s, most states considered, but then abandoned, anti-drug education in schools out of fear that knowledge about drugs would lead to experimentation and addiction. By the middle of the century, according to Laurie LaChance in *Alcohol and Drug Use Among Adolescents*, "any drug use was considered to be pathological."

However, medical and scientific discoveries in the past several decades have lent support to the disease model of dependency. Researchers have found that the brains of addicts are different from those of people who are not dependent on drugs, tobacco, or alcohol. In an article for the magazine *Current Health*, Melissa Abramovitz explains: "Addictive drugs change the brain. Most doctors now agree that addiction is a disease, not a weakness." Drugs such as cocaine and heroin activate the brain's reward system, causing the user to experience pleasure and euphoria. Repeated abuse of these substances can alter the brain's chemistry, which makes people suffering from chemical dependency respond more intensely to drugs. In addition, increased levels of tolerance require that drug users take more of the substance in order to feel the same euphoria, which raises the likelihood of an overdose. Adolescents are most at risk because their brains undergo many changes during puberty. They are also more vulnerable to addiction because they are more likely than adults to take risks. Many youth are also genetically predisposed to addiction.

Not everyone has embraced this view of dependency. Among its doubters are Sally Satel, a lecturer at the Yale University School of Medicine. Writing for the journal *Public Interest*, she contends that there have been no scientific studies linking drug exposure with changes in the brain. Satel also argues that the brain-disease model ignores the importance of the criminal justice system in ending drug addiction. She writes: "By downplaying the volitional dimension of addiction, the brain-disease model detracts from the great promise of strategies and therapies that rely on sanctions and rewards to shape self-control."

Despite these qualms, many people support medically-based drug treatment over jail. In the opinion of the Physician Leadership on National Drug Policy: "Addiction to illegal drugs is a chronic illness. . . . Enhanced medical and public health approaches are the most effective method of reducing harmful use of illegal drugs." Thus, like other diseases, chemical dependency is often best treated with drugs, among them methadone, which reduces the craving for heroin, and naltrexone, which blocks the effects of heroin on the brain's receptors and is effective in treating alcohol dependency. Because one element of chemical dependency is the inability to decrease drug use despite knowledge of its deleterious effects, counseling and behavioral modification are also critical facets of drug treatment.

The success of Proposition 36 may determine whether popular support for drug treatment continues. In March 2002, the Drug Policy Alliance (DPA) issued an evaluation of the effects of Proposition 36 in seven California counties. The alliance found that the Substance Abuse and Crime Prevention Act was "on the path to fulfill its promise to the voters to reduce the rates of drug addiction and crime by diverting offenders to drug treatment." According to the report, 9,500 drug offenders had been referred to treatments in the first six months of the act's implementation. The DPA believes that the number of qualifying individuals will gradually decrease as participants in programs defeat their drug addictions and get out from under the auspices of the criminal justice system.

Americans have debated the causes and treatments of chemical dependency for centuries. In *Chemical Dependency: Opposing Viewpoints*, the authors consider these arguments and related controversies in the following chapters: Is Chemical Dependency a Serious Problem? What Causes Chemical Dependency? What Drug Treatment and Prevention Programs Are Effective? Should Drug Laws Be Reformed? In their viewpoints, the authors provide a better understanding of a problem that affects millions of people.

CHAPTER 1

Is Chemical Dependency a Serious Problem?

Chapter Preface

Since the 1990s there has been a sharp increase in the abuse of what are known as "club drugs." Originally used largely in urban areas, especially among gay men, these drugs, in particular Ecstasy, have become increasingly popular among adolescents, who are not always aware of the dangers posed by these substances. According to a National Institute on Drug Abuse survey, 3.4 million Americans age twelve or over have tried Ecstasy at least once. In addition, 2.8 percent of twelfth-graders polled in 2001 had taken Ecstasy during the previous month.

Ecstasy, or MDMA (methylenedioxymethamphetamine), is a stimulant that is typically taken in pill form. The drug causes the brain to release serotonin, a neurotransmitter that controls mood. Its users reportedly experience euphoria and enhanced mental and emotional clarity. However, these purportedly positive experiences are accompanied by dangerous side effects, among them brain damage, anxiety, paranoia, nausea, chills, and increases in blood pressure and heart rate. The Drug Abuse Warning Network reports that Ecstasy-related health problems resulted in more than four thousand five hundred visits to the emergency room in 2000.

The side effects of Ecstasy can also be fatal. Abusers at clubs often dance to the point of dehydration, which can lead to death due to failure of the kidneys and the cardiovascular system. Ecstasy use has also caused seizures, strokes, and heart attacks. The drug has contributed to at least ten deaths in Maryland and eight deaths in Miami. Also dangerous is counterfeit Ecstasy (paramethoxyamphetamine and paramethoxymethamphetamine), which has been linked to deaths in Florida and Illinois. In addition, Ecstasy pills are often laced with cocaine, PCP, or other drugs, which can increase the drug's risks. It is therefore not surprising that Alan Leshner, the director of the National Institute on Drug Abuse, has stated, "MDMA is not a benign drug. In fact, all of the studies conducted to date in both animals and more recently in humans, confirm that club drugs, particularly MDMA, are not harmless 'fun party drugs' as they are often portrayed." Ecstasy is not the only drug whose popularity has raised questions about the spread of drug abuse in the United States. In the following chapter, the authors debate whether chemical dependency is a serious problem or if the extent and dangers of drug abuse have been exaggerated.

"Youth drug use rates today are the product of attitudinal trends that experts say began in the late 1980s."

Teen Drug Abuse Is a Serious Problem

Barry McCaffrey

In the following viewpoint, Barry McCaffrey contends that a significant percentage of adolescents are abusing illegal drugs, tobacco, and alcohol. According to McCaffrey, one out of every four high school seniors has used an illegal drug at least once during the past month, while approximately 12 percent of eighth graders have used drugs in the same time period. McCaffrey argues that while marijuana is the most frequently abused drug, the increased rates of heroin, cocaine, and hallucinogenic use are of particular concern because of the deadly nature of these substances. He also asserts that millions of teenagers smoke and drink regularly, both of which are risk factors for drug use. McCaffrey was the director of the Office of National Drug Control Policy during President Bill Clinton's administration.

As you read, consider the following questions:
1. According to studies, during what time periods are adolescents most likely to get into trouble with drugs?
2. What is the mean age of first use of hallucinogens, as stated by the National Household Survey?
3. What does McCaffrey believe is a "self-fulfilling prophecy"?

Barry McCaffrey, testimony before the Senate Committee on the Judiciary, June 17, 1998.

America's most vital resources are our young people. They are literally our future. We have no higher moral obligation than to safeguard the lives and dreams of our nation's children. The dangers of illegal drug use pose the greatest risk facing the generation of youth coming of age in the next millennium. One-in-four twelfth graders is a current user of illegal drugs (past month).

The Demographics of Drug Use

Among eighth graders the percentage of current users stands at one-in-eight. The 1996 National Household Survey (NHSDA) found that nine percent of twelve to seventeen year olds are current drug users. While this number is well below the 1979 peak of 16.3 percent, it is still alarmingly higher than the 1992 low of 5.3 percent. A survey conducted by the Columbia University Center on Addiction and Substance Abuse found that 41 percent of teens reported attending a party where marijuana was available, and 30 percent had seen drugs sold at schools.

Moreover, because the number of young people in this nation will dramatically increase with the next generation (the "Millennium Generation"), even if we reduce the percentage of young people actively using drugs, we remain likely to be faced with increasing raw numbers of young people with initial exposure to drugs. Between 1997 and 2007, public high school enrollment will increase by roughly 13 percent. Beyond 2007, long-range projections are that births will increase by 4.2 million in 2010 and 4.6 million in 2020. Unless we can prevent this next generation from ever turning to drugs, we will face a far larger problem than we see today.

Growing numbers of two-wage-earner households and single parent families are increasing the ranks of latch-key kids. Studies show that the time periods when children are out of school and without adult supervision are the hours when they are most likely to get into trouble with drugs and other high risk behaviors. Adult—and in particular parental—involvement is critical to reducing youth drug use. With more parents working, the role of the extended family, coaches, law enforcement officers, clergy, health professionals, and other youth mentors becomes even more critical.

Marijuana, Heroin, and Cocaine Use

Among young people, marijuana continues to be the most frequently used illegal drug. The 1997 *Monitoring the Future Study* (*MTF*) found that 49.6 percent of high school seniors reported having tried marijuana at least once—up from 41 percent in 1995. After six years of steady increases, the rate of current marijuana use among eighth graders fell from 11.3 percent in 1996 to 10.2 percent in 1997. However, this small shift must be put into perspective. Modest declines notwithstanding, roughly one-in-ten eighth graders have tried marijuana. We should not miss the point. Roughly 40 percent of youngsters, ages 15 to 19, who enter drug treatment have marijuana as the primary drug of abuse. This is a dangerous drug, particularly for adolescents.

Increasing rates of heroin use among youth are truly frightening. While heroin use among young people remains quite low, use among teens rose significantly in eighth, tenth, and twelfth grades during the 1990s. (However, past-year heroin use decreased among 8th graders and remained stable among 10th and 12th graders between 1996 and 1997.) In every grade (eighth, tenth and twelfth), 2.1 percent of students have tried heroin. A frightening statistic for such a horrible drug. The heroin now being sold on America's streets has increased in purity, which allows for the drug to be snorted or smoked, as well as injected. The availability of alternative means of delivery, which young people see as less risky and more appealing than injecting, has played a major role in the increases in youth heroin use. The number of young heroin users who snort or smoke the drug continues to rise across the nation. The NHSDA found that the average age of initiation for heroin had fallen from 27.3 years old in 1988 to 19.3 in 1995.

Cocaine use, though not prevalent among young people, is far too frequent an experience for our youth. The 1997 *MTF* survey found that the proportion of students reporting use of powder cocaine in the past year to be 2.2 percent, 4.1 percent, and 5 percent in grades eight, ten, and twelve, respectively. This rate represents a leveling-off in eighth-grade use and no change in tenth and twelfth grades. Among eighth graders, perceived risk also stabilized in 1997, and

Reported Drug, Alcohol, and Cigarette Use in Last 30 Days Among High School Seniors, by Type of Drug, United States, 1984–1996

Percent who used in last 30 days

Type of Drug	Class of 1984 (N=15,900)	Class of 1985 (N=16,000)	Class of 1986 (N=15,200)	Class of 1987 (N=16,300)	Class of 1988 (N=16,300)	Class of 1989 (N=16,700)	Class of 1990 (N=15,200)	Class of 1991 (N=15,000)	Class of 1992 (N=15,800)	Class of 1993 (N=16,300)	Class of 1994 (N=15,400)	Class of 1995 (N=15,400)	Class of 1996 (N=14,300)
Marijuana/hashish	25.2%	25.7%	23.4%	21.0%	18.0%	16.7%	14.0%	13.8%	11.9%	15.5%	19.0%	21.2%	21.9%
Inhalants	1.9	2.2	2.5	2.8	2.6	2.3	2.7	2.4	2.3	2.5	2.7	3.2	2.5
Adjusted	2.6	3.0	3.2	3.5	3.0	2.7	2.9	2.6	2.5	2.8	2.9	3.5	2.9
Amyl and butyl nitrites	1.4	1.6	1.3	1.3	0.6	0.6	0.6	0.4	0.3	0.6	0.4	0.4	0.7
Hallucinogens	2.6	2.5	2.5	2.5	2.2	2.2	2.2	2.2	2.1	2.7	3.1	4.4	3.5
Adjusted	3.2	3.8	3.5	2.8	2.3	2.9	2.3	2.4	2.3	3.3	3.2	4.6	3.8
LSD	1.5	1.6	1.7	1.8	1.8	1.8	1.9	1.9	2.0	2.4	2.6	4.0	2.5
PCP	1.0	1.6	1.3	0.6	0.3	1.4	0.4	0.5	0.6	1.0	0.7	0.6	1.3
Cocaine	5.8	6.7	6.2	4.3	3.4	2.8	1.9	1.4	1.3	1.3	1.5	1.8	2.0
Crack	NA	NA	NA	1.3	1.6	1.4	0.7	0.7	0.6	0.7	0.8	1.0	1.0
Other cocaine	NA	NA	NA	4.1	3.2	1.9	1.7	1.2	1.0	1.2	1.3	1.3	1.6
Heroin	0.3	0.3	0.2	0.2	0.2	0.3	0.2	0.2	0.3	0.2	0.3	0.6	0.5
Other opiates	1.8	2.3	2.0	1.8	1.6	1.6	1.5	1.1	1.2	1.3	1.5	1.8	2.0

Adapted from Lloyd D. Johnston, Patrick M. O'Malley, and Jerald G. Bachman, *National Survey Results on Drug Use from The Monitoring the Future Study, 1975–1996*, vol. 1, Secondary School Students (Washington, D.C.: U.S. Government Printing Office, 1997).

20

disapproval of use increased—both after an earlier erosion in these attitudes. The 1996 NHSDA found current use among twelve to seventeen year olds to be 0.6 percent, twice the rate of 1992 yet substantially lower than the 1.9 percent reported in 1985. The fact that young people are still experimenting with cocaine underscores the need for effective prevention. This requirement is substantiated by NHSDA finding of a steady decline in the mean age of first use from 22.6 years in 1990 to 19.1 years in 1995. Crack cocaine use, according to *MTF*, leveled-off in the eighth, tenth, and twelfth grades during the first half of the 1990s.

Abuse of Other Substances

The 1997 *MTF* reports that inhalant use is most common in the eighth grade where 5.6 percent used it on a past-month basis and 11.8 percent did so on a past-year basis. Inhalants can be deadly, even with first-time use, and often represent the initial experience with illicit substances. Current use of stimulants (a category that includes methamphetamine) declined among eighth graders (from 4.6 to 3.8 percent) and tenth-graders (from 5.5 percent to 5.1 percent) and increased among twelfth graders (from 4.1 to 4.8 percent). Ethnographers continue to report 'cafeteria use'—the proclivity to consume any readily available hallucinogenic, stimulant or sedative drugs like ketamine, LSD, MDMA, and GHB. Young people take mood-altering pills in night clubs knowing neither what the drug is nor the dangers posed by its use alone or in combination with alcohol or other drugs. Treatment providers have noted increasing poly-drug use among young people throughout the country. NHSDA reports that the mean age of first use of hallucinogens was 17.7 years in 1995, the lowest figure since 1976. These numbers in large part reflect the continuing popularity of drugs, such as methamphetamines, inhalants, and psychotherapeutics (tranquilizers, sedatives, analgesics, or stimulants), within the youth "club scene." Raves—late night dances, in which drug use is a prominent feature—remain popular among young people. The "rave scene," which is now firmly rooted in popular culture—from MTV to music, to movies—has been a major contributing factor to youth drug deaths in Orlando, Florida, and escalating drug use in other regions.

The dangers for today's young people are particularly pronounced. The purity of heroin available on our streets is much higher than ever before. Higher purity means higher risks. "Speedballing"—combining heroin with cocaine—is increasingly common. Treatment providers report that 75 percent of clients in heroin treatment report cocaine abuse as well. In California, methamphetamine use is so widespread that the drug is no longer considered an emerging threat—it has arrived. Meth use on the East Coast is a growing problem. Ketamine, GHB and Rohypnol—all "club drugs"—are also emerging threats from coast to coast. Marijuana use among young people is increasing and indications are that the age of initiation is falling. For example, treatment providers report that over one-third of all clients receiving treatment for marijuana abuse are under the age of twenty.

Youth drug use rates for illegal drugs, such as marijuana and heroin, are also linked to the high percentage of our young people who use tobacco. Overall, 4.5 million young people under the age of eighteen now smoke; every day another three thousand adolescents become regular smokers. One-third of these new smokers will die from tobacco-related disease. According to the NHSDA, an estimated 18 percent of young people ages twelve to seventeen are current smokers. Daily cigarette smoking rose 43 percent among high school seniors between 1992 and 1997. The 1997 *MTF* similarly found that daily cigarette smoking among high school seniors reached its highest level (24.6 percent) since 1979. Among eighth graders, this study found that nine percent report smoking on a daily basis; 3.5 percent smoke a half-pack or more per day. Study after study finds a high correlation between young people who start smoking during their adolescence and then turn to other more dangerous drugs.

Similar concerns are raised by the rate of underage drinking. In 1997, the *MTF* found that 15 percent of eighth, 25 percent of tenth, and 31 percent of twelfth graders reported binge drinking in the two weeks prior to being interviewed. The 1996 NHSDA found past-month alcohol use among 18.8 percent of twelve to seventeen year olds. New research indicates that the younger the age of drinking onset, the greater the chance that an individual at some point in life will develop a clinically defined alcohol disorder. Young people who began drinking before age fifteen were four times more likely to develop alcohol dependence than those who began drinking at age twenty-one. Among eighteen to twenty-five year olds, the number jumps to almost six-in-ten. Between 1996 and 1997, the incidence of "binge" drinking rose by 15 percent among twelve to seventeen year olds. "Heavy" drinking has increased by almost 7 percent during the same period. Here again, underage alcohol use is a risk factor that correlates with higher incidences of drug use among young people.

Deadly Attitudes

Youth drug use rates today are the product of attitudinal trends that experts say began in the late 1980s. (By 1990 at the latest, young people's perceptions of risk in drug use peaked and began to fall.) Most disturbingly, even though the average young person is not using drugs, almost one-in-four twelfth graders say that "most or all" of their friends use illegal drugs. They tend to believe that abstinence from drug use places them in the minority—something all children fear. The danger is that this false impression becomes a self-fulfilling prophecy. This misperception puts tremendous pressure on the average youth to yield to peer and societal pressures to experiment with drugs—oftentimes a tragic decision.

"The 'teenage heroin resurgence' repeatedly trumpeted in headlines and drug-war alarms is fabricated."

Teen Drug Abuse Has Been Exaggerated

Mike Males

Despite the claims of the media and drug-war advocates, chemical dependency is chiefly an adult, not adolescent, problem, Mike Males claims in the following viewpoint. According to Males, teenage drug use—in particular heroin use—is a small percentage of America's drug problem. He argues that teenagers are far more likely to drink or smoke than take illegal drugs, thus making drug laws targeting adolescents unnecessary and ineffective. Males is a freelance writer whose books include *The Scapegoat Generation: America's War on Adolescents* and *Framing Youth: Ten Myths About the Next Generation.*

As you read, consider the following questions:

1. How many Americans received hospital treatment for drug-related ailments in 1999?
2. According to statistics cited by Males, what percentage of twelve- to seventeen-year-olds tried heroin during 1999?
3. In the author's opinion, what must politicians do in order to end the drug crisis?

Mike Males, "Fighting a War Armed with Baby-Boomer Myths," *Los Angeles Times*, February 4, 2001, p. M2. Copyright © 2001 by *Los Angeles Times*. Reproduced by permission.

Remarks by [now retired] drug czar Barry McCaffrey and accolades for the Steven Soderbergh film "Traffic" by drug-policy reform groups frame a vigorous drug-war debate—circa 1970. Thirty years ago McCaffrey's goal to save our children from their own drug use might have been relevant. So, too, "Traffic" 's scenes of the daughter of the film's drug czar sampling heroin in response to the hypocrisies of liquor-swilling and pill-popping grown-ups.

The Chief Myth of the Drug War

But these vintage baby-boom notions have little to do with today's drug realities. On one side, the rhetorical distortions and misdirected policies of the Office of National Drug Control Policy squandered billions of dollars and locked up millions of drug users—and the United States is enduring the worst drug-abuse crisis in its history. As McCaffrey leaves office, the federal Drug Abuse Warning Network reports that drug abuse soared to record peaks in 1999: An estimated 555,000 Americans were treated in hospitals for drug-related visits; at least 11,600 died from overdoses. On the other side, reformers seeking to decriminalize marijuana and relax drug policies perpetrate so many drug-war myths that they reinforce hard-line attitudes even as they win minor improvements.

The chief drug-war myth is the "demographic scapegoat." Wars against drugs (including Prohibition) always seek to link feared drugs to feared populations: the Chinese and opium; Mexicans and marijuana; black musicians and cocaine; and Catholic immigrants and alcohol. Today's war on drugs sustains itself by depicting white suburban teenagers menaced by inner-city youths' habits. No matter who peddles it, this image is unreal. In truth, the drug-abuse crisis chiefly concerns aging baby boomers, mostly whites. A high schooler is five times more likely to have heroin-, cocaine- or methamphetamine-addicted parents than the other way around; far more senior citizens than teenagers die from illegal drugs. Accordingly, a "war on drugs" that truly cared about protecting children would make treating parents' addictions its top priority.

The "teenage heroin resurgence" repeatedly trumpeted in

headlines and drug-war alarms is fabricated; it shows up nowhere in death, hospital, treatment or survey records. The Drug Abuse Warning Network's most hospital survey [from 2000] reports 84,500 treatments for heroin abuse nationwide in 1999; just 700 of these were for adolescents. Of 4,800 Americans who died from heroin abuse, only 33 were under 18 years old. Press panics over supposed teenage heroin outbreaks in Portland and Seattle [in summer 2000] collapsed when the Centers for Disease Control and Prevention reported the average overdoser was 40 years old.

Teenage "heroin epidemics" breathlessly clarioned in some California cities are refuted by hospital records that show just nine of San Francisco's 3,100 emergency treatments for heroin overdoses in 1999 were teenagers, as were 17 of San Diego's 1,100 and two of Los Angeles's 2,950. Why aren't there more teen heroin casualties? Few use it. The National Household Survey on Drug Abuse, released in September 2000, showed that .2% of 12- to 17-year-olds had used heroin at any time in the previous year. Nor are the few heroin initiators getting younger (most remain over 21).

Teenagers and Soft Drug Use

There are preppie kids who smoke heroin, as "Traffic" depicts, but their numbers pale beside the tens of thousands of baby boomers whose addictions are rooted in the Vietnam era. Four-fifths of California's heroin decedents are over the age of 30, and three-fourths of them are white, a quintessentially mainstream demographic neither drug warrior nor drug reformer wishes to target. Thus, policy debate and cinematic representations promote a comfortable myth: Baby-boom drug days are behind us.

Similarly, drug-reform publications such as *DrugSense Weekly* allege an "increase in heroin use among our youth" to indict the drug war. Mike Gray, author of "Drug Crazy," and other reformers claim decriminalizing and regulating marijuana for adults would make it harder for teenagers to get. Ridiculous. The 1999 National Household Survey on Drug Abuse reports 12- to 17-year-olds use legal, adult-regulated cigarettes and alcohol 100 times more than they use heroin; two to three times more teens drink or smoke than use the most popular illicit, marijuana. Teenagers can get alcohol and drugs whenever they want them, yet suffer very low casualties. Drug reformers' own research gospel, the Lindesmith Center's exhaustive "Marijuana Myths, Marijuana Facts," finds no scientific reason why teenagers should be banned from using marijuana that would not also apply to adults. In short, teenagers are not the issue.

Marijuana and Teen Drug Use

According to the most recent literature from the National Institute on Drug Abuse (NIDA), the majority of marijuana users do not become dependent or move on to use other illegal drugs. This stands to reason when one realizes that an estimated 70 million Americans have experimented with marijuana at some point in their lives, the majority of whom never went on to use cocaine. Therefore, while it may be true that some cocaine users did first use marijuana as an adolescent, the far more important fact is that the overwhelming number of teen marijuana users never go on to use cocaine or any other illegal narcotic.

Paul Armentano, *Freedom@NORML*, September 1996.

Drug policy will change only when compelling new information is introduced. That means discarding first-wave baby-boomer drug images and moving toward second-generation realities. Throughout the Western world, young people are reacting against their parents' hard-drug abuse by patronizing softer drugs such as beer and marijuana. It's understandable that baby boomers would indulge moral panic over any drug use by kids while denying their own middle-aged drug woes, but these illusions should not govern 2000-era drug policy.

Success in the Netherlands

The Netherlands' 1976 Dutch Opium Act reforms recognized that modern soft-drug use by young people is separate from the midlife hard-drug crisis. Dutch studies showed that marijuana and hashish use was unrelated to hard-drug abuse, except among a small fraction already inclined to addiction. These conclusions were confirmed by the National Household Survey on Drug Abuse analysts and long-term studies by University of California researchers. True, most drug abusers first tried drugs in their youth, as did most non-abusers. But 90% of the 160 million American adults who used marijuana or alcohol during adolescence did not find them "gateways" to later addiction.

The Netherlands' reforms stressing public-health strategies to contain hard-drug abuse, coupled with tolerance for marijuana use by adults and teenagers, has produced a spectacular benefit: a 65% decline in heroin deaths since 1980 (while U.S. heroin death rates doubled).

Whether or not Dutch-style reforms are feasible here, the U.S. will not reduce its worst-ever drug-abuse crisis until politicians radically revamp the Office of National Drug Control Policy and the facile demographic scapegoating of young people. Yet, because drug reformers, copying drug-war hard-liners, increasingly promote their agendas by exploiting youth as fear-invoking symbols in today's anachronistic "debate," genuine reform seems remote.

"Active cigarette smoking has been causally linked to lung cancer and associated with an array of other diseases."

Smoking Causes Significant Health Problems

Alicia M. Lukachko and Elizabeth M. Whelan

In the following viewpoint, Alicia M. Lukachko and Elizabeth M. Whelan respond to an article written by Robert Levy and Rosalind Marimont. Lukachko and Whelan contend that, despite Levy and Marimont's claims, cigarette smoking causes serious health problems for smokers and people exposed to secondhand smoke. Among these illnesses, according to the authors, are emphysema, respiratory illnesses, and vision and hearing problems; these diseases result in as many as 700,000 deaths each year. The authors maintain that numerous studies have corroborated the link between smoking and diseases. Lukachko is the former assistant director of public health at the American Council on Science and Health (ACSH); Whelan is the president of ACSH.

As you read, consider the following questions:

1. What are some of the cardiovascular diseases with which cigarette smoking has been associated, as stated by the authors?
2. Why do Lukachko and Whelan find Levy and Marimont's arguments about secondhand smoke simplistic?
3. According to the authors, why is it difficult to calculate the number of deaths attributable to cigarette smoking?

Alicia M. Lukachko and Elizabeth M. Whelan, "A Critical Assessment," *Regulation*, vol. 23, 2000, pp. 2–4. Copyright © 2000 by The Cato Institute. Reproduced by permission.

Cigarette smoking has been recognized as a leading cause of disease and death for at least 40 years. Few subjects have received such thorough and extensive scientific scrutiny by both governmental and independent bodies. Thousands of scientific studies have confirmed that smoking is a major health hazard. Besides the relationship between smoking and disease, many studies have found that the overall death rate among smokers is two to three times greater than that of non-smokers. Cigarettes also contain nicotine, a chemical proven to be highly addictive (which internal tobacco-industry documents have acknowledged).

Despite overwhelming evidence to the contrary, [Robert] Levy and [Rosalind] Marimont [in *Regulation*, Fall 1998] state that the hazards of smoking remain largely speculative. They allege that the "war on smoking started with a kernel of truth—that cigarettes are a high risk factor for lung cancer." Ironically, it is Levy and Marimont's article that contains only a kernel of truth about the risks of smoking. In fact, active cigarette smoking has been causally linked to lung cancer and associated with an array of other diseases; specifically:

The Health Hazards of Smoking

• Cigarette smoking is a principal cause of cancer of the esophagus, larynx, lip, mouth, pharynx, tongue, kidney, pancreas, urinary bladder, and uterine cervix.

• Cigarette smoking has been identified as a major cause of cardiovascular disease, including atherosclerosis, coronary heart disease (angina and heart attack), stroke, sudden death, and aortic aneurysm.

• Cigarette smoking causes chronic obstructive lung disease (emphysema, chronic bronchitis, and related conditions). Smokers have been found to suffer more respiratory problems (such as colds, pneumonia, influenza, and bronchitis) and their recovery from those illnesses is slower.

• For men under age 65, smoking has been shown to be an independent risk factor for impotence, including erectile dysfunction. For women, smoking can impair fertility, induce premature menopause and spontaneous abortion, and lead to a host of complications of pregnancy and childbirth.

• Cigarette smoking increases the risk for osteoporosis (a

reduction in bone mass) and periodontal (gum) disease.

• Smoking precipitates vision problems, including blindness secondary to cataracts and macular degeneration, and premature hearing loss.

• Smokers face a significantly greater chance than do nonsmokers of suffering complications during and after surgery. Evidence suggests that smoking also increases the risk for other diseases, such as rheumatoid arthritis, and cancers of the prostate and stomach. Those relationships, however, have not yet been scientifically established.

Preliminary research also indicates that cigarette smoking may be associated with reduced risk for endometrial cancer and Parkinson's disease. Yet the harmful effects of cigarette smoking dramatically outweigh any of its potential benefits.

The Dangers of Secondhand Smoke

A mounting body of scientific research reveals that exposure to environmental tobacco smoke (ETS) also poses health risks. The most common and firmly established adverse health effects associated with exposure to ETS are irritation of the eyes, nose, and respiratory tract; exacerbation of asthma and emphysema; and increased susceptibility to respiratory infections. Furthermore, studies have consistently shown that ETS contributes to lung cancer and heart disease. (See *Environmental Tobacco Smoke, Health Risk or Health Hype?*, a 1999 report by the American Council on Science and Health.)

As Levy and Marimont's article itself illustrates, concerns about secondhand smoke extend far beyond public health. The political implications of finding a causal association between ETS and disease have fueled long and bitter struggles between pro- and anti-tobacco organizations and individuals. In an effort to resist the trend toward indoor-smoking restrictions and to allay public fears, some parties, including the tobacco industry, have argued that ETS does not pose a "meaningful" lung cancer risk—and therefore does not present a threat to public health.

Similarly, authors Levy and Marimont focus their arguments about secondhand smoke exclusively on lung cancer in an attempt to dismiss all of the health effects associated with ETS. Their argument is simplistic, as it ignores ETS-related health risks other than lung cancer—heart disease and respiratory illnesses, for example—that should also be considered when developing public health policy.

Evaluating the Effects of Smoking

Scientists rely on epidemiology—the study of the distribution and determinants of disease frequency—to determine whether a factor, such as cigarette smoking, causes a particular health outcome, that is, disease or death. They begin by suggesting and then establishing an association

The best way to evaluate the effect of smoking on health is to compare groups of smokers with groups of nonsmokers to assess the differences between them (if any) in health outcomes. Researchers try to ensure that, aside from smoking, the smokers and nonsmokers have similar characteristics, so that differences in health outcomes are more likely attributable to smoking than to other factors. Statistical analysis of the research data can help to explain differences in health outcomes attributable to smoking, even where there are dissimilarities between the groups.

Tobacco's Young Victims

Tobacco may not kill until middle age or later but in a sense, it chooses its victims young. Some 90 percent of all smokers have their first cigarette by age 20. And the younger a person is at the time of that first cigarette, the more confirmed and heavier a smoker that person is likely to be as an adult. Consequently, children and young adults who smoke are at a much higher risk for later disease than are people who take up the habit when they are older. On average, smokers who light their first cigarette at age 25 lose about 4 years of life; those who start at age 15 lose 8 years.

Anne Platt McGinn, *World Watch*, July/August 1997.

When an association is found between smoking and disease or death, researchers must determine whether the apparent association is valid. A valid association is unlikely to be the result of chance, bias on the part of researchers or study participants, or confounders—other factors that caused the disease and are independently associated with smoking.

Statistical tests are routinely applied to research findings to assess the probability that the results are "statistically significant" and not merely coincidental. A test for statistical significance takes into account such factors as the number of persons examined (sample size) and the strength of the association between the exposure and the health outcome. Generally, the larger the sample size and the stronger the association, the more likely it is that the results will be found to be significant.

Even if a result is statistically significant, bias and potential confounders must be addressed to demonstrate a valid association. Furthermore, a statistically significant finding does not alone confirm a causal relationship. To conclude that smoking causes a particular disease, researchers must assess the relationship against five criteria:

Five Key Principles

Strength of the association found between smoking and disease. Relative risk is the ratio of disease among smokers to disease among nonsmokers. A relative risk of 1 indicates that there is no association between the exposure and the outcome. The closer relative risk is to 1, the smaller or weaker the association.

A relative risk of 2, for example, would indicate that smokers are twice as likely as nonsmokers to develop the health outcome under study (e.g., death from heart disease). The larger the relative risk, the less likely an association can be attributed solely to bias or confounders. But a small relative risk does not exclude the possibility of a causal relationship, nor does it preclude the possibility that the relative risk is statistically significant.

Consistency of the finding across studies. If several well-designed studies replicate a finding, the more likely it is that the relationship being studied is real. As stated previously, the enormous body of research on the health effects of smoking corroborates the relationship between smoking and disease.

Biological plausibility of the hypothesis. The relationship between an exposure and a disease must be consistent with what is known about biology and the disease. Much is understood about the biological mechanisms by which smoking causes disease, though more remains to be learned. It is known that cigarette smoke contains approximately 4,000 chemical components, many of which are toxins and some of which are human carcinogens.

Presence of a dose-response relationship. In a dose-response relationship, risk increases with the degree of exposure. Many studies have shown that increases in the duration of cigarette use and number of cigarettes smoked increase the risk for smoking-related disease and death.

Sequence of cause and effect. The exposure or hypothesized cause must precede the effect. There is ample research to affirm that cigarette use precedes adverse health outcomes. . . .

Calculating the Death Toll

The number of deaths attributable to cigarette smoking may be thought of as the reduction in the number of deaths that would obtain if no one had ever smoked. That reduction is essentially estimated in the following way:

1. Apply death rates for smoking-related diseases among representative nonsmokers to the entire population. That gives the number of deaths expected if everyone were a nonsmoker.
2. Subtract the expected number of deaths from the actual number of deaths.

The calculation is complicated by the fact that the many people who have smoked and quit have a greater risk of smoking-related disease than do people who have never smoked. Therefore, some formulas, such as that used by the Centers for Disease Control and Prevention (CDC), distinguish between current smokers, former smokers, and "never-smokers" in estimating the incidence of smoking-related deaths.

Estimates of the death toll from smoking can vary widely, depending on what diseases are considered smoking-related, the data sources used, the control for confounding variables (e.g., age), and variations in formulas.

For more than two decades, the U.S. government has been estimating the number of Americans who die prematurely from smoking. The government currently estimates that about 430,000 deaths occur each year in the United States as a result of cigarette smoking. (Higher estimates fall in the range of 600,000 to 700,000 annual deaths.)

"Damage done from alcohol [and] damage done from drugs . . . are vastly more important than the damage done from tobacco."

Smoking-Related Health Problems Have Been Exaggerated

Robert A. Levy, interviewed by Stephen Goode

The health risks of smoking have been overstated, Robert A. Levy claims in the following viewpoint. Although Levy acknowledges that there are medical problems associated with smoking, he maintains that dependency on tobacco is less damaging than alcohol or drug dependency and that tobacco's link to certain diseases cannot be proven statistically. Levy contends that antitobacco lawsuits pose a greater risk than smoking because they eliminate personal responsibility and lead to government infringement on individual rights. Levy is an attorney and a senior fellow in constitutional studies at Cato Institute, a libertarian think tank; Stephen Goode is a senior writer for *Insight*.

As you read, consider the following questions:
1. According to Levy, what problems are associated with epidemiological studies?
2. Why does Levy believe tobacco is less dangerous than drugs or alcohol?
3. According to Levy, what do the tobacco lawsuits teach children?

Robert A. Levy, "Cato's Levy Challenges Federal Tobacco Myths," *Insight*, vol. 16, January 31, 2000, pp. 37–38. Copyright © 2002 by News World Communications, Inc. Reproduced by permission.

Insight: In "Lies, Damned Lies, & 400,000 Smoking-Related Deaths" [from the fall 1998 issue of Regulation] you concluded that the government's estimate of 400,000 annual deaths due to cigarette smoking is unreliable. What's wrong with that figure?

The Relative Risk of Smoking

Robert A. Levy: According to the Centers for Disease Control and Prevention, tobacco-related diseases are those in which the rate of risk among smokers is higher than among nonsmokers. But epidemiologists will tell you without exception, I think, that "simply higher" is not enough. In most studies, the requirement to show a correlation is that the risk be three or four times as high.

The reason for requiring a relative risk rate among smokers of three or four times what it is among nonsmokers before categorizing a disease as smoking-related is that epidemiological studies are subject to all sorts of statistical problems.

There's the problem of sampling error. There is the problem of bias. The third problem is what epidemiologists call "compounding variables": that is the failure to take into account variables that are correlated both with the disease and with smoking. The obvious one in this case is socioeconomic status, as smokers tend to be less affluent than nonsmokers. So because of the problems of sampling, bias and of compounding variables, epidemiologists insist that to categorize a disease as tobacco-related the disease has to have a relative risk among smokers that is three or four times that among nonsmokers.

The relative risk of smoking for many types of heart disease is less than 2-to-1, and if you eliminate even those that are just below 2-to-1 you reduce the estimated number of tobacco-related deaths by about 55 to 60 percent.

We know that smokers are poorer than nonsmokers, have worse nutritional intake, typically have less exercise and less education. Those factors contribute to the contraction of various diseases described as smoking-related. To suggest that the entire incidence among smokers is because these people smoke is to ignore that they share exposure to many other characteristics that also impact health.

Manipulating Statistics

What's the reason for the distortion?

Underlying such manipulation of statistics one often finds a political agenda, a public-policy agenda, which seeks to convince the public that something is a terrible scourge—and to do so even if the polemic violates the standards and principles of statistics and epidemiology.

This is not to say that tobacco is not a problem. Tobacco is clearly a problem. The evidence is overwhelming that use of tobacco can cause lung cancer, emphysema, bronchitis. But with respect to other diseases its role is less certain. This causes us to ask whether the government is lying to us in presenting these kinds of statistics, because, if it is, that has implications.

What implications?

We've seen what happened with antitobacco lawsuits. They've morphed now into antigun litigation. Shortly, it will be the HMOs [health-maintenance organizations] under attack. Who knows what will be next? Fatty foods and alcohol are other obvious candidates for such government-sponsored litigation. The corruption of science for political ends is destructive to a free society and dangerous to citizens who want their government to refrain from activities that intrude upon the rights of people to make their own choices.

Data are being massaged so as to produce outcomes that the litigants find congenial; whether those outcomes are supported by the data is disregarded. I think that's exactly what happened in the tobacco wars.

Tobacco Versus Other Substances

Tobacco is a problem about which 45 million people decided that it's too dangerous and they quit smoking. For more than 35 years now we've had warnings on every single pack of cigarettes that has been sold legally in the United States. It's a product about which the risks are well-known. Those risks, in fact, have been exaggerated and this has meant that public policy has focused on the unreal, exaggerated risks to the exclusion of some other sources of risk that might better have targeted.

Damage done from alcohol, damage done from drugs,

from suicide and particularly from homicide all are vastly more important than the damage done from tobacco, I think. Tobacco is not an intoxicant. It doesn't cause crime except for those people involved in avoiding taxes or regulation of a product whose price has been pushed through the roof by legislation, taxation and regulation. Tobacco doesn't, as do drugs and alcohol, result in spousal abuse and child abuse. It doesn't break up families. It doesn't result in unemployment.

Secondhand Smoke and Junk Science

Since the Environmental Protection Agency listed second-hand smoke as a first-class human carcinogen in 1993, numerous eminent scientists have expressed skepticism. They include epidemiologists Dimitrios Trichopoulos of the Harvard School of Public Health and Alvan Feinstein of Yale Medical School. Dr. Philippe Shubik, editor in chief of *Teratogenesis, Carcinogenesis and Mutagenesis*, published at Oxford University, contrasts cigarette smoking—"an unequivocal human cancer hazard"—with environmental smoke. Officially designating the latter a human carcinogen, he writes, "is not only unjustified but establishes a scientifically unsound principle."

In other words, anti-tobacco activists who ascribe murderous carcinogenic qualities to secondhand smoke are engaging in junk science and propaganda, just as were the pro-tobacco spokesmen who denied the carcinogenic properties of smoking.

Dennis Prager, *Weekly Standard*, July 20, 1998.

Nor does tobacco result in the deaths of young people. Drugs and alcohol, suicide and homicide are killing young people in the prime of life, with decades of life left. The average age of what are called tobacco-related deaths is 72. Those years lost after 72 are important, but they're not so significant, not of the same magnitude, as years lost to the young. . . .

The Tobacco Lawsuit Epidemic

How can the enormous power of government in [tobacco lawsuits] be brought under control?

A solution is a "lose-you-pay" system. When the state is a plaintiff in a civil case—and I use the word "state" broadly to encompass government at all levels—we ought to require that it pay if it loses. The government has coercive taxing power behind it [which, for one thing, supplies an almost unlimited supply of funds], so when the government is the plaintiff in a civil case, we need this extra protection against the abuse of the government's power.

Is there any means to bring under control the huge fees plaintiff lawyers have been getting in these cases?

Yes. We could prohibit contingency fees for cases when the state is plaintiff. I don't have any objection to contingency fees arranged by private litigants. But when you combine the state as plaintiff and a contingency-fee contract, that is abusive. You can imagine the abuse you would have if you hired an attorney general and paid him for each indictment he got a grand jury to hand down or if you paid state troopers based on how many speeding tickets they handed out. But that's exactly what's happened with private attorneys hired by the state in these civil cases. We've seen legal fees in Texas of $92,000 an hour!

Meanwhile, we've been eliminating personal responsibility by saying a person's not responsible for his or her own choice to smoke.

We actually eliminated assumption of risk. In Florida, Maryland and Vermont they did it by statute. They actually said in their statutes that the tobacco industry may not use assumption of risk as a defense. Secondly, they eliminated the rule of causation. The tobacco industry, they said, could not require the states in court to show a link between any smoker's conduct and the disease. The only evidence the states had to produce were these macrostatistics we've talked about showing the higher incidence of various diseases among smokers than nonsmokers. So it was all washed away in one stroke of the pen, all the rules of causation and the assumption of risk.

That is more destructive than the impact of cigarettes themselves! Basically, we're now telling kids two things: First, you can change the rules of the game after the game has begun because all these rules were retroactive. Second, you can go out and engage in risky behavior and if it doesn't turn out like you wanted, you can force the cost onto some third party.

"*Approximately 9 million Americans used prescription drugs for non-medical purposes in 1999.*"

Prescription Drug Abuse Is a Growing Problem

Michelle Meadows

In the following viewpoint, Michelle Meadows asserts that prescription drug abuse is an increasingly serious problem. Meadows maintains that people who abuse prescription drugs, such as OxyContin and Ritalin, are seeking psychological effects while avoiding the stigma of "street drugs." However, she contends that prescription drug abuse, like heroin abuse, can be fatal and can encourage criminal and irresponsible behavior. Meadows is a writer for *FDA Consumer*, a publication of the Food and Drug Administration.

As you read, consider the following questions:
1. What are the factors that cause prescription drug abuse, according to Meadows?
2. As stated by the author, why did many people believe that OxyContin would pose a lower risk for abuse?
3. What is the preoccupation associated with psychological addiction, according to the author?

Michelle Meadows, "Prescription Drug Use and Abuse," *FDA Consumer*, vol. 35, September 2001, p. 18.

It was supposed to be a short course of treatment with tranquilizers after the death of her infant son 15 years ago. But Lynn Ray, 46, of Germantown, Maryland, says her abuse of the anti-anxiety drug Xanax and other prescription drugs led to a long struggle with addiction that nearly ruined her life.

Tranquilizers, which slow down the central nervous system and cause drowsiness, numbed Ray's agony, helped her sleep, and untied the relentless knot in her stomach. Soon, even if her doctor had prescribed one pill in an eight-hour period, she took two or three in an attempt to intensify the calming effect of the drug. When the doctor stopped writing prescriptions for her and encouraged grief counseling, Ray began doctor-shopping—going from doctor to doctor, fabricating panic attacks, backaches, migraines, and other ailments that would get her multiple prescriptions for tranquilizers and pain killers. "I became a very good actress," Ray says. "I thought I needed these drugs no matter what, even if I had to bamboozle the doctors to get them."

The Causes of Prescription Drug Abuse

Most patients take medicine responsibly, but approximately 9 million Americans used prescription drugs for non-medical purposes in 1999, according to the National Institute on Drug Abuse (NIDA).

Non-medical purposes include misusing prescription drugs for recreation and for psychic effects—to get high, to have fun, to get a lift, or to calm down.

Experts stress that prescription drug abuse isn't about bad drugs or even bad people. It involves a complex web of factors, including the power of addiction, misperceptions about drug abuse, and the difficulty both patients and doctors have discussing the topic.

There is also the delicate balance of curbing criminal activity related to drug abuse while making sure that people with legitimate health needs can still access care, says Alan I. Leshner, Ph.D., director of NIDA. "We recognize the very real issue that millions of lives are improved because of prescription drugs—the same drugs that are sometimes abused," he says.

Consequences of Abuse

Ray had convinced herself that abusing prescription drugs was safer than abusing heroin, marijuana, and other "street drugs." "I would never do those," she says. "I figured I had a prescription for what I was doing, which made it OK."

Scott Walker, program director for substance abuse at the Mountain Comprehensive Care Center in Prestonsburg, Kentucky, says he hears that rationalization over and over. "Some people tell themselves they aren't using something old Joe cooked up in a garage somewhere," Walker says. They may figure a legitimate manufacturer made this, "so what could be the harm?"

As Ray's life unraveled, she found out the harm can be great, whether you're using heroin or sleeping pills. She lost her job as a computer programmer after repeatedly showing up late for work and falling asleep at her desk. Her son, a preteen at the time, couldn't understand her erratic behavior and didn't want anything to do with her.

Then in 1995, she crashed her car three times in one month while under the influence of tranquilizers and painkillers, seriously injuring others each time. Her driver's license was revoked, and she served a one-year jail sentence in 1998. "I will always know in my heart that I could have killed those people," she says. "It doesn't matter that I didn't kill them; it matters that I could have."

Walker says that roughly half of the people undergoing substance abuse treatment at Mountain Comprehensive Care Center come after realizing that they found themselves in a hole too deep to get out of on their own. The other half, like Ray, come because of some criminal charge related to drug possession or drug use.

The OxyContin Crisis

OxyContin (oxycodone), a controlled drug approved in 1995 to treat chronic, moderate-to-severe pain, has received considerable attention because of deaths and crimes associated with its abuse. OxyContin is a morphine-like narcotic that contains a high dose of oxycodone. Manufactured by Purdue Pharma, Stamford, Connecticut, the drug was originally believed to pose a lower risk for abuse because it is a controlled-release drug designed to be taken orally and swallowed whole, says Deborah Leiderman, M.D., director of the Food and Drug Administration's controlled substance staff. The drug's active ingredient, oxycodone, is slowly released over a 12-hour period. "But the safety of the drug is based on taking the drug exactly as intended," she says.

"Yes, Billy, but Mr. Phillips pushes legal drugs."

Downes. © 1998 by Nick Downes. Reprinted with permission.

Abusers sometimes disrupt the time-release formula of the drug to speed up absorption, often chewing the tablets, crushing them and snorting the powder, or dissolving them in water and injecting the drug to get a fast high. Abusers have also used OxyContin with other painkillers, alcohol, and marijuana. Several deaths have resulted, mostly in rural areas of the Eastern United States, especially in Virginia and West Virginia.

Other products containing oxycodone such as Percodan and Percocet have also been abused over the years. Abuse of opiates is not new; what's new is the recent surge in local epidemics of opiate abuse.

The most highly abused stimulants are illicit drugs, including cocaine and methamphetamines. There also have been recent reports of Ritalin (methylphenidate) abuse among middle and high school students. The drug, which produces effects more potent than caffeine and less potent than amphetamine, is prescribed to treat attention-deficit/hyperactivity disorder and other conditions. But some have used it to suppress their appetite or to stay awake while studying. The Drug Enforcement Agency (DEA) lists Ritalin as a "drug of concern" and reports that some abusers have dissolved the tablets in water and injected the mixture, which can block small blood vessels and damage the lungs and retina of the eye.

Complexities of Addiction

It's not that potentially addictive medications shouldn't be used, says Richard Brown, M.D., M.P.H., associate professor of family medicine at the University of Wisconsin Medical school. "They have an important place in the treatment of debilitating conditions." According to NIDA, drug addiction—characterized by drug craving that is out of control—is actually uncommon among people who use drugs as prescribed.

NIDA, along with several health organizations, has launched a national initiative to educate the public about the dangers of the non-medical use of prescription drugs, and the potential for abuse and addiction. With psychological addiction, there is a preoccupation with obtaining and using drugs that persists despite the consequences. Psychological addiction is distinct from physical dependence and tolerance, but the presence of these problems can complicate the treatment of addiction, says Alice Young, Ph.D., a professor in the department of psychology at Wayne State University in Detroit. "It is true that both psychological addiction and physical dependence can happen together," she says, "but they are not the same."

Young says that physical dependence, which is sometimes unavoidable, develops when an individual is exposed to a drug at a high enough dose for long enough that the body adapts and develops a tolerance for the drug. This means that higher doses are needed to achieve a drug's original effects. "If the patient stops taking the drug, then withdrawal will occur," Young says.

But the development of physical dependence doesn't necessarily lead to addiction in all cases, she explains. "It means that the individual can't just stop taking the drug; the dose has to be tapered," a method to gradually decrease a drug's amount over time to prevent withdrawal reactions.

In addition to promoting public education, NIDA's initiative will foster new research on why certain people become addicted, says Leshner. "Some choose prescription drugs as the drug of choice, and others become addicted inadvertently," he says. "We want to learn more about what makes some people more likely to stray from the prescribed plan than others." NIDA also will support research into the mechanisms by which certain substances produce addiction.

"*A national [prescription drug abuse]
epidemic? No. Not even close.*"

The Media Have Exaggerated the Prescription Drug Abuse Crisis

Tom Shales

The media have exaggerated and encouraged the problem of prescription drug abuse, Tom Shales contends in the following viewpoint. He claims that television newscasts are more interested in presenting stories that both demonize and glamorize drugs such as OxyContin than in offering accurate information on these drugs' medical benefits. In fact, OxyContin is extremely effective as a pain reliever for those suffering intense pain. Unfortunately, Shales maintains, sensationalized news reports may scare doctors away from prescribing OxyContin and other useful drugs. Tom Shales is a television critic and editor for the *Washington Post*.

As you read, consider the following questions:
1. Why does Shales believe television coverage of prescription drug abuse encourages further abuse?
2. According to Robin Hogen, why is OxyContin abuse confined primarily to five states?
3. What is the "Pain Community," as defined by Shales?

Tom Shales, "Drug Abuse—Or TV News Abuse," *Electronic Media*, vol. 20, March 26, 2001, p. 4. Copyright © 2001 by *Electronic Media*. Reproduced by permission.

TV news doesn't really cover the field of medicine. Instead it goes about the business of fomenting hysteria. Sometimes it's a kind of benign hysteria, the careless spreading of false hope by reporting on some small advance in scientific research that may or may not result in a medical breakthrough three, six, 10 or 20 years down the pike. Don't hold your breath, as the saying goes.

But what the TV news boys and girls really love is a hot juicy story that spreads fear and loathing about drugs and their dangers, real or imagined. Apparently it's good box-office—that is, good for ratings—to air stories that demonize a particular drug and at the same time help to popularize it.

News Stories Encourage Abuse

Every network news department has now done a story or two on a drug called OxyContin, a high-powered painkiller prescribed for the most severe cases of suffering; cancer patients are among those most likely to have it prescribed and to consider it a godsend. But it turns out that in some areas where the usual hard-core recreational drugs like crack cocaine are in short supply, substance abusers have found a way to get high on OxyContin. They grind it up into powder and snort it or make it soluble and inject it into their veins.

A national epidemic? No. Not even close. But TV newscasts have tried to portray it that way in stories filled with hype and half-truths. And in the course of "reporting" on abuse of the drug, they've all aired how-to pieces that include handy, easy-to-follow instructions on the correct abuse procedure. They tell you how to get high. Then the correspondents do follow-up reports expressing shock and dismay that the abuse is becoming more popular.

Yeah, more kids are using the drug to get high because they heard about it and even saw how to use it on the evening news.

The hysteria gets whipped up by each succeeding piece until we reach the point, noted in an "NBC Nightly News" report [in March 2001] that some doctors are reluctant to prescribe the drug because it's suddenly got this "bad" reputation. Meanwhile, kids who might never have dreamed of using it to get high are breaking into pharmacies and stealing it or mugging patients as they leave pharmacies after having their legitimate prescriptions filled.

OxyContin's Dangers Have Been Overstated

"We are the drug du jour," laments Robin Hogen, executive director of public affairs for Purdue Pharma, the company that makes the drug. For those with intractable pain, with pain that has resisted other medications, OxyContin has been a blessing. But media hysteria threatens that, at least until the panic spotlight moves on to some other medication.

When I was in Los Angeles, every TV station was doing stories on Vicodin and how for celebrities it's the drug of choice for recreational use. These reports made Vicodin sound fashionable, cool, chic—irresistible. In the pursuit of ratings, the reporters were encouraging impressionable viewers to get hold of some of that Vicodin and tie one on. You won't just be high, you'll be hip. Oddly, OxyContin wasn't mentioned. Maybe it will be the drug du jour in Los Angeles when the Vicodin stories start falling flat.

Confusion About Addiction

The fear of opioid addiction in the face of evidence to the contrary is based largely on people's confusion about what addiction actually means. Many people erroneously equate addiction with physical dependence. People who take opioids for a prolonged period of time usually do develop physical dependence, which means that they would experience withdrawal symptoms—nausea, vomiting, cramps, tremors—if the medication were abruptly discontinued. But this is a normal state of adaptation that can occur with drugs other than opioids.

Tufts University Health & Nutrition Letter, April 2002.

TV reporters have been "hysterical from Day One," Hogen says, in reporting on abuses of OxyContin and on deaths allegedly caused by overdoses. Well, not "caused by." The reporters are careful. They usually say "linked to." Even that may be a stretch of the facts. It's been repeatedly reported that the drug can be linked to 59 deaths in Kentucky in 2000 and 2001. Why Kentucky, of all places? That's part of the story the reporters usually leave out. Even ignoring that, the figure may very well be bogus. Once one reporter uses it, all other reporters feel free to use it without double-checking. But there is no hard evidence that OxyContin played a key role in 59 Kentuckians keeling over. David Jones, an official with the Kentucky State Medical Examiner's office, looked into the claim and wrote a letter to Purdue Pharma:

> I am unaware of any reliable data in Kentucky that proves OxyContin is causing a lot of deaths. In the State Medical Examiner's Office, we are seeing an increase in the number of deaths from ingesting several different prescription drugs and mixing them with alcohol. OxyContin is sometimes one of these drugs.

Creating a National Problem

What's happened, Hogen says, is that a regional story has been inflated into a national one by TV journalists. He says abuse of OxyContin is confined mainly to "rural pockets" in five states: Maine, West Virginia, Virginia, Alabama and Kentucky. Why rural areas of those states? "Because the people who abuse drugs there can't get heroin or crack cocaine the way people in big cities can," Hogen says. "It's part of the economics of the drug business. The abuse is mainly in poor rural communities where there is high unemployment and high substance abuse already."

As the TV reporters have made vividly clear, manipulating the drug by crushing it (thus bypassing a time-release feature) and then injecting it can give a sudden and drastically euphoric high. They usually trot out an abuser to describe how delicious and wonderful the high can be, thus making it sound still more enticing to what we might call the Drug Abuse Community.

But there is also in America something called a Pain Community. These are people suffering intensely from pain or involved in research to find more and better ways to control it. OxyContin gives effective pain relief for 12 hours with no euphoria involved, Hogen says, but TV news is giving it a reputation as a cheap kick for drugcrazed thrill-seekers.

Could the network news departments turn a regional problem into a national problem by continuing with these alarmist reports? "Absolutely," Hogen says. "None of these clowns on television are reporting the beneficial aspects of the drug. Only the abuse. They are scaring pharmacists, scaring doctors and scaring patients."

Contrary to reports, the drug is not new but was introduced in 1995. Finding a way to abuse it has been a fairly recent occurrence, apparently. Hogen says stories about the abuse just happened to break during the first week of the February Sweeps. What luck for TV newscasters. "They jumped on it as if they had discovered gold," he says. Each network in turn dutifully did its report, with each reporter trying to top the previous guy's piece by making the drug sound deadlier, the high sound higher, the hazards more hazardous. It isn't hard to imagine news directors at local stations throughout the country now wondering aloud at staff meetings why the station hasn't had its own report on the big OxyContin scare. You can't just let a nice panicky rabble-rouser like that slip through your fingers. Then more kids and other substance abusers get exposed to the story and the drug leaps forward in popularity and infamy. There is, apparently, no epidemic of OxyContin abuse. And while movie stars may currently favor Vicodin as their high of choice, there's no epidemic of Vicodin abuse either.

What's epidemic is bad journalism. But you won't see Dan Rather or Tom Brokaw or Peter Jennings doing any stories on that.

Periodical Bibliography

The following articles have been selected to supplement the diverse views presented in this chapter.

Paul H. Brodish   "The 'Smoking' Unborn," *Priorities for Health*, volume 11, number 1, 1999.

Jane E. Brody   "Misunderstood Opioids and Needless Pain," *New York Times*, January 22, 2002.

Ann B. Bruner and Marc Fishman   "Adolescents and Illicit Drug Use," *Journal of the American Medical Association*, August 19, 1998.

Suzanne Fields   "Deadly Heroin Makes a Comeback," *Insight on the News*, October 4–11, 1999.

Robert Levy and Rosalind Marimont   "Lies, Damned Lies, & 400,000 Smoking-Related Deaths," *Regulation*, Fall 1998.

Mike Males   "Raving Junk," *Extra!*, December 2000.

Anne Platt McGinn   "The Nicotine Cartel," *World Watch*, July/August 1997.

Evelyn Nieves   "Heroin, an Old Nemesis, Makes an Encore," *New York Times*, January 9, 2001.

Dennis Prager   "The Soul-Corrupting Anti-Tobacco Crusade," *Weekly Standard*, July 20, 1998.

Peter Reuter   "Drug Use Measures: What Are They Really Telling Us?" *National Institute of Justice Journal*, April 1999.

Debra Rosenberg   "Oxy's Offspring," *Newsweek*, April 22, 2002.

Don Sloan   "Getting High in America," *Political Affairs*, December 2000.

Brian Vastag   "Mixed Message on Prescription Drug Abuse," *Journal of the American Medical Association*, May 2, 2001.

CHAPTER 2

What Causes Chemical Dependency?

Chapter Preface

Many people concerned about the problem of drug abuse in the United States contend that Americans, especially teenagers, are influenced by positive portrayals of drug use, drinking, and smoking in movies, television, and music. If their assessment is true, then it is not so farfetched to believe that popular culture can discourage substance abuse as well. In 1997 President Bill Clinton's administration sought to prove that theory.

The White House and the television networks negotiated an agreement under which the networks could place anti-drug messages in their television shows in lieu of airing anti-drug advertisements. The Office of National Drug Control Policy (ONDCP) reviewed the scripts and made suggestions to improve the drug-related plotlines. Shows with episodes approved under the arrangement included *ER*, *The Drew Carey Show*, and *The Practice*. Among the issues addressed in these and other shows were teenage drug use, drug testing, and the dangers of driving under the influence of alcohol and marijuana.

The Office of National Drug Control Policy then assigned a financial value to each show, based on the show's length, popularity, and the quality of its message. For example, *ER's* episodes earned NBC $1.4 million worth of advertising time, which the network could then use to air nongovernment commercials. In the administration's opinion, the success of these messages was well worth the financial tradeoff. Barry McCaffrey, who was the drug czar during Bill Clinton's administration, claimed that the antidrug messages contributed to a 13 percent decline in teenage drug use.

When the press learned of the agreement in late 1999, they decried the government's efforts to limit and influence the content of television shows. In an article for the online magazine *Salon*, Andrew Jay Schwartzman, president of the Media Access Project, a public interest law firm, is quoted as saying "To turn over content control to the federal government for a modest price is an outrageous abandonment of the First Amendment." The *Washington Post* questioned the White House's lack of openness about the arrangement, arguing in an editorial that such secrecy deceived television viewers. The newspaper writes, "Unlike viewers of antidrug ads, viewers of these programs don't know that they are receiving government-sponsored political messages. It's kind of like commercial product placement—only the product is White House spin."

The theory that the media can influence personal behavior such as drug abuse has been popular for many decades. Other causes of drug abuse include genetics and the influence of parents and friends. In the following chapter, the authors explore other causes of chemical dependency.

| *"The addicted brain is distinctly different from the nonaddicted brain."*

Addiction Is a Brain Disease

Alan Leshner

In the following viewpoint, Alan Leshner maintains that drug addiction is a chronic illness that is linked to changes in brain structure. According to Leshner, drugs activate a pathway in the brain; activation of that pathway, known as the mesolimbic reward system, prompts a dependency on these substances. Leshner concludes that by understanding the connection between the brain and addiction, society can develop more effective treatments and public health strategies. Leshner is the director of the National Institute on Drug Abuse.

As you read, consider the following questions:
1. In Leshner's opinion, what is the most common view of drug addicts?
2. According to the author, in what ways are addicted brains different from nonaddicted brains?
3. What does Leshner consider "a reasonable standard for treatment success"?

Alan Leshner, "Addiction Is a Brain Disease—And It Matters," *National Institute of Justice Journal*, October 1998, pp. 2–6. Copyright © 1998 by *National Institute of Justice Journal*. Reproduced by permission.

D ramatic advances over the past two decades in both the neurosciences and the behavioral sciences have revolutionized our understanding of drug abuse and addiction. Scientists have identified neural circuits that are involved in the actions of every known drug of abuse, and they have specified common pathways that are affected by almost all such drugs. Research has also begun to reveal major differences between the brains of addicted and nonaddicted individuals and to indicate some common elements of addiction, regardless of the substance.

However, a dramatic lag or gap exists between these advances in science and their appreciation by the general public or their application in either practice or public policy settings. For example, many, perhaps most, people see drug abuse and addiction as social problems, to be handled only with social solutions, particularly through the criminal justice system. On the other hand, science has taught that drug abuse and addiction are as much health problems as they are social problems. The consequence of this perception gap is a significant delay in gaining control over the drug abuse problem.

Unique Factors

Part of the lag and resultant disconnect comes from the normal delay in transferring any scientific knowledge into practice and policy. However, other factors unique to the drug abuse arena compound the problem, such as:

• *The tremendous stigma attached to being a drug user or, worse, an addict.* The most beneficent public view of drug addicts is as victims of their societal situation. However, the more common view is that drug addicts are weak or bad people, unwilling to lead moral lives and control their behavior and gratifications. To the contrary, addiction is actually a chronic, relapsing illness, characterized by compulsive drug seeking and use. The gulf in implications between the "bad person" view and the "chronic illness sufferer" view is tremendous. As just one example, many people believe that addicted individuals do not even deserve treatment. This stigma, and the underlying moralistic tone, is a significant overlay on all decisions related to drug use and drug users.

• *Ingrained ideologies.* Some who work in the drug abuse prevention and addiction treatment fields also hold ingrained ideologies that, although usually different in origin and form from the ideologies of the general public, can be just as problematic. For example, many drug abuse workers are themselves former drug users who have had successful treatment experiences with a particular treatment method. They therefore may zealously defend a single approach, even in the face of contradictory scientific evidence. In fact, many drug abuse treatments have been shown to be effective through clinical trials.

These difficulties notwithstanding, we can and must bridge this informational disconnect if we are to make real progress in controlling drug abuse and addiction. It is time to replace ideology with science.

Addiction as a Health Issue

What has the science shown and what are the implications? At the most general level, research has shown that drug abuse is a dual-edged health issue as well as a social issue. Drugs have well-known and severe negative consequences for abusers' health, both mental and physical. But drug abuse and addiction also have tremendous implications for the health of the public, since drug use, directly or indirectly, is now a major vector for the transmission of many serious infectious diseases, particularly HIV/AIDS, hepatitis, and tuberculosis—and for the infliction of violence as well. Because addiction is such a complex and pervasive health issue, overall strategies must encompass a committed public health approach, including extensive education and prevention efforts, treatment, and research.

Science is providing the basis for such public health approaches. For example, two large sets of multisite studies have demonstrated the effectiveness of well-delineated outreach strategies in modifying the HIV-risk behaviors of addicted individuals, even if they continue to use drugs and do not want to enter treatment. This runs counter to the broadly held view that addicts are so incapacitated by drugs that they are unable to modify any of their behaviors. It also suggests a base for improved strategies for reducing the negative health consequences of injection drug use for the individual and for society.

Outdated Thinking

Scientific research and clinical experience have taught us much about what really matters in addiction and where we need to concentrate our clinical and policy efforts. However, too often the focus is on the wrong aspects of addiction, and efforts to deal with this difficult issue can be badly misguided.

Any discussion about psychoactive drugs inevitably turns to the question of whether a particular drug is physically or psychologically addicting. In essence, this issue revolves around whether dramatic physical withdrawal symptoms occur when an individual stops taking a drug—what is typically called physical dependence by professionals in the field. The assumption that often follows is that the more dramatic the

---

Drugs and Brain Chemicals

The discovery of the endorphins (the brain's own opiates) in the 1970s brought home the possibility that drugs may compensate for an inborn or acquired chemical deficiency. These endorphins are chemical messengers made in nervous tissue and released in response to painful, frightening, or satisfying experiences (e.g. sexual intercourse). They turn off aversive (unpleasant) messages and mediate reward. Intuitively, it is highly desirable to have an abundant supply at your disposal. If you are deficient in endorphins and happen to be exposed to opioids, or short of dopamine and exposed to amphetamine, it seems logical to suppose that you will be particularly sensitive to the rewarding or aversion-reducing effect. We know from research into depression that people can be naturally low in certain chemical messengers (for example, serotonin), and that this may increase their susceptibility to suicide. Perhaps this deficiency could be genetically programmed, an idea which finds some support in animal experiments. This finding has prompted the suggestion that some addicts may be no more to blame for their state than diabetics. Just as a diabetic needs insulin to maintain normal functioning, perhaps the endorphin-deficient junkie needs heroin and the dopamine-starved cocaine snorter must have his stimulant.

Philip Robson, *Forbidden Drugs*, 1999.

---

physical withdrawal symptoms, the more serious or dangerous the drug must be.

This thinking is outdated. From both clinical and policy perspectives, it does not matter much what physical withdrawal symptoms, if any, occur. First, even the florid withdrawal symptoms of heroin addiction can now be easily managed with appropriate medications. Second, and more important, many of the most addicting and dangerous drugs do not produce very severe physical symptoms upon withdrawal. Crack cocaine and methamphetamine are clear examples. Both are highly addicting, but cessation of their use produces very few physical withdrawal symptoms, certainly nothing like the physical symptoms accompanying alcohol or heroin withdrawal.

What does matter tremendously is whether a drug causes what we now know to be the essence of addiction: compulsive drug seeking and use, even in the face of negative health and social consequences. These are the characteristics that ultimately matter most to the patient and where treatment efforts should be directed. These elements also are responsible for the massive health and social problems that drug addiction brings in its wake.

The Addict's Brain

Although each drug that has been studied has some idiosyncratic mechanisms of action, virtually all drugs of abuse have common effects, either directly or indirectly, on a single pathway deep within the brain, the mesolimbic reward system. Activation of this system appears to be a common element in what keeps drug users taking drugs. This is not unique to any one drug; all addictive substances affect this circuit.

Not only does acute drug use modify brain function in critical ways, but prolonged drug use causes pervasive changes in brain function that persist long after the individual stops taking the drug. Significant effects of chronic use have been identified for many drugs at all levels: molecular, cellular, structural, and functional. The addicted brain is distinctly different from the nonaddicted brain, as manifested by changes in brain metabolic activity, receptor availability, gene expression, and responsiveness to environmental cues. Some of these long-lasting brain changes are idiosyncratic to specific drugs, whereas others are common to many different drugs. We can actually see these changes through use of recently developed technologies, such as positron emission tomography. The common brain effects of addicting substances suggest common brain mechanisms underlying all addictions.

That addiction is so clearly tied to changes in brain structure and function is what makes it, fundamentally, a brain disease. A metaphorical switch in the brain seems to be thrown following prolonged drug use. Initially, drug use is a voluntary behavior, but as that switch is thrown, the individual moves into the state of addiction, characterized by compulsive drug seeking and use.

Understanding that addiction is, at its core, a consequence of fundamental changes in brain function means that a major goal of treatment must be either to reverse or to compensate for those brain changes. This could be accomplished through either medications or behavioral treatments (behavioral treatments alter brain function in other psychobiological disorders). Elucidation of the biology underlying the metaphorical switch is key to the development of more effective treatments, particularly antiaddiction medications.

Of course, addiction is not that simple. Addiction is not just a brain disease. It is a brain disease for which the social contexts in which it both has developed and is expressed are critically important. The case of the many thousands of returning Vietnam war veterans who were addicted to heroin illustrates this point clearly. In contrast to addicts on the streets of America, it was relatively easy to treat the returning veterans' addictions. This success was possible because they had become addicted while in an almost totally different setting from the one to which they returned. At home in the United States, they were exposed to very few of the conditioned environmental cues that had initially been associated with their drug use in Vietnam. Exposure to those conditioned cues can be a major factor in causing persistent or recurrent drug cravings and drug use relapses even after successful treatment.

The implications are obvious. If we understand addiction as a prototypical psychobiological illness, with critical biological, behavioral, and social context components, our treatment strategies must include biological, behavioral, and social context elements. Not only must the underlying brain disease be treated, but the behavioral and social cue components must also be addressed, just as they are with many other brain diseases, including stroke, schizophrenia, and Alzheimer's disease.

Addiction is rarely an acute illness. For most people, it is a chronic, relapsing disorder. Total abstinence for the rest of one's life is a relatively rare outcome from a single treatment episode. Relapses are more the norm. Thus, addiction must be approached more like other chronic illnesses—diabetes, chronic hypertension—than like an acute illness, such as a bacterial infection or a broken bone. This has tremendous implications for how we evaluate treatment effectiveness and treatment outcomes. Viewing addiction as a chronic, relapsing disorder means that a good treatment outcome—and the most reasonable expectation—is a significant decrease in drug use and long periods of abstinence, with only occasional relapses. Thus, a reasonable standard for treatment success is not curing the illness but managing it, as is the case for other chronic illnesses.

Lessons to Be Learned

Addiction as a chronic, relapsing disease of the brain is a totally new concept for much of the general public, for many policymakers, and, sadly, for many health care professionals. Many of the implications have been discussed above. But there are others.

At the policy level, understanding the importance of drug use and addiction for the health of individuals and of the public affects many of our overall public health strategies. An accurate understanding of the nature of drug abuse and addiction also affects our criminal justice strategies. For example, if we know criminals are also drug addicted, it is no longer reasonable to simply incarcerate them. If they have a brain disease, imprisoning them without treatment will be futile. If they are left untreated, their crime and drug use recidivism rates are frighteningly high. However, if addicted criminals are treated while in prison, both types of recidivism can be reduced dramatically. It is therefore counterproductive not to treat addicts while they are in prison.

At an even more general level, understanding addiction as a brain disease also affects how society approaches and deals with addicted individuals. We need to face the fact that even if the condition initially comes about because of a voluntary behavior (drug use), an addict's brain is different from a nonaddict's brain and the addicted individual must be dealt with as if he or she is in a different brain state. We have learned to deal with people in different brain states for schizophrenia and Alzheimer's disease. As recently as the beginning of [the twentieth] century, we were still putting individuals with schizophrenia in prison-like asylums, whereas now we know they require medical treatments. We now need to see the addict as someone whose mind (read: brain) has been altered fundamentally by drugs. Treatment is required to deal with the altered brain function and the concomitant behavioral and social functioning components of the illness.

Understanding addiction as a brain disease explains in part why historic policy strategies focusing solely on the social or criminal justice aspects of drug use and addiction have been unsuccessful. They are missing at least half of the issue. If the brain is the core of the problem, attending to it needs to be a core part of the solution.

"Addiction is a function of a person, rather than simply a physical state."

Addiction Is Not a Brain Disease

Sally Satel

Drug addiction is a behavioral phenomenon, not a brain disease, Sally Satel argues in the following viewpoint. She contends that the idea that chemical dependency is involuntary ignores the fact that addicts are capable of self-control. According to Satel, the fact that addicts seek treatment and try to quit drugs when they recognize the negative consequences of drug use is proof that chemical dependency is a voluntary decision that can be overcome by behavioral therapies. Satel is a lecturer at the Yale University School of Medicine.

As you read, consider the following questions:
1. In Satel's view, why should politicians resist the "medicalized portrait" of drug addiction?
2. Which correlation claimed by brain disease advocates does Satel say has not been clearly demonstrated?
3. According to the author, how do cocaine and heroin addicts differ?

Sally Satel, "Is Drug Addiction a Brain Disease?" *Drug Addiction and Drug Policy: The Struggle to Control Dependence*, edited by Philip B. Heymann and William N. Brownsberger. Cambridge, MA: Harvard University Press, 2001. Copyright © 2001 by the President and Fellows of Harvard College. Reproduced by permission.

M ore than one hundred substance-abuse experts gathered in Chantilly, Virginia, in November 1995, for a meeting called by the government's top research agency on drug abuse. A major topic was whether the agency, the National Institute on Drug Abuse (NIDA), which is part of the National Institutes of Health, should declare drug addiction a disease of the brain. The experts—academics, public health workers, state officials, and others—said yes, overwhelmingly.

A Widespread Movement

At the time that answer was controversial, but since then the notion of addiction as a brain disease has become widespread, thanks in large measure to a full-blown public-education campaign by NIDA. Waged in editorial boardrooms, town hall gatherings, and Capitol Hill briefings and hearings, the campaign reached its climax in the spring of 1998 when the media personality Bill Moyers catapulted the brain-disease concept into millions of living rooms with his five-part television special. Using imaging technology, Moyers showed viewers eye-catching pictures of addicts' brains under Positron Emission Tomography (PET) scan. The cocaine-damaged parts of the brain were "lit up"—an "image of desire," one researcher called it.

Dramatic visuals are seductive and lend scientific credibility to NIDA's position, but politicians should resist this medicalized portrait for at least two reasons. First, it appears to reduce a complex human activity to a slice of damaged brain tissue. Second, and more important, it vastly underplays the reality that much of addictive behavior is voluntary.

The idea of a "no-fault" disease did not originate at NIDA. For the last decade or so it has been vigorously promoted by mental-health advocates working to transform the public's understanding of severe mental illness. Until the early 1980s, remnants of the psychiatric profession and much of the public were still inclined to blame parents for their children's serious mental problems. Then accumulating neuroscientific discoveries began to show, irrefutably, that schizophrenia was marked by measurable abnormalities of brain structure and function. Diseases like schizophrenia and manic-depressive illness were products of a defective brain, not bad parenting.

The mental health movement has drawn momentum from the 20-year-old National Alliance for the Mentally Ill (NAMI), the nation's largest grassroots advocacy organization for people with severe psychiatric disorders and their families. NAMI has mounted a vigorous anti-stigma campaign—slogan: mental illnesses are brain diseases—that has sought to capture public attention through television exposure, publicized opinion polls and surveys, star-studded fundraisers, and frequent congressional testimony. Its success can be seen in the increasing media coverage of severe mental illness, sympathetic made-for-TV specials about the mentally ill, and the widespread assumption, usually explicitly stated by reporters, that these conditions have a biological origin.

Redefining Addiction

While some of those experts who met in Chantilly would say that emphasizing the role of will, or choice, is just an excuse to criminalize addiction, the experience of actually treating addicts suggests that such an orientation provides grounds for therapeutic optimism. It means that the addict is capable of self-control—a much more encouraging conclusion than one could ever draw from a brain-bound, involuntary model of addiction.

The brain-disease model leads us down a narrow clinical path. Since it implies that addicts cannot stop using drugs until their brain chemistry is back to normal, it overemphasizes the value of pharmaceutical intervention. At the same time, because the model also says that addiction is a "chronic and relapsing" condition, it diverts attention from truly promising behavioral therapies that challenge the inevitability of relapse by holding patients accountable for their choices.

Getting a purchase on the true nature of addiction is difficult. Even the definition is elusive. For example, addiction can be defined by pathological state (as a brain disease if affected neurons are examined); by "cure" (as a spiritual disease if vanquished through religious conversion); or by psychodynamics (as a matter of voluntary behavior if addicts are given incentives that successfully shape their actions). Yet when clinicians, scientists, and policymakers are confronted by such definitional choices, it makes the most sense to settle on the one with the greatest clinical utility. In what follows, therefore, I will argue the virtues of thinking about addiction as a primary, though modifiable, behavioral phenomenon, rather than simply as a brain disease. That is, addiction is a function of a person, rather than simply a physical state.

The Brain Disease Argument

An NIDA article entitled "Addiction Is a Brain Disease, and It Matters," published in October 1997 in the prestigious journal *Science*, summarizes the evidence that long-term exposure to drugs produces addiction—that is, the compulsion to take drugs—by eliciting changes in specific neurons in the central nervous system. Because these changes are presumed to be irreversible, the addict is perpetually at risk for relapse. The article states:

> Virtually all drugs of abuse have common effects, either directly or indirectly, on a single pathway deep within the brain. Activation of this pathway [the mesolimbic reward system] appears to be a common element in what keeps drug users taking drugs . . . The addicted brain is distinctly different from the non-addicted brain, as manifested by changes in metabolic activity, receptor availability, gene expression and responsiveness to environmental cues . . . That addiction is tied to changes in brain structure and function is what makes it, fundamentally, a brain disease.

The psychiatrist and molecular biologist Steven Hyman puts the biology in a larger, evolutionary context. "Adaptive emotional circuits make brains vulnerable to drug addiction," he says, "because certain addictive drugs mimic or enhance the actions of neurotransmitters used by those circuits." By the time drugs and alcohol have become objects of intense desire, Hyman's research suggests, they've commandeered key motivational circuits away from normal human pleasures, like sex and eating. On a cellular level, bombardment by drugs and alcohol produces chronic adaptations in the neurons of the key circuits, leading to dependence, a state in which the brain "demands" that the addict get high. This is a distinctly different understanding of disease from that promoted by Alcoholics Anonymous, the institution most responsible for popularizing the disease concept of addiction.

In AA, disease is employed as a metaphor for loss of control. Thus members might say, "I am unable to drink or take drugs because I have a disease that leads me to lose control when I do." And even though AA assumes that the inability to stop drinking once started is biologically driven, it does not allow this to overshadow its central belief that addiction is a symptom of a spiritual defect. The goal is sobriety through personal growth and the practice of honesty and humility.

The brain-disease advocates are operating in an entirely different frame of reference. Within it they have stipulated that "addiction" means compulsive drug-taking driven by drug-induced brain changes. They assume a correlation between drug-taking behavior and PET scan appearance, though such a correlation has yet to be clearly demonstrated, and they speculate, on the basis of preliminary evidence, that subtle changes persist for years. The assumption seems to be that the neuroscience of addiction will give rise to pharmaceutical remedies. But to date the search for a cocaine medication has come up empty. And the disposition to use drugs commonly persists among heroin addicts even after treatment with the best medication for normalizing the compulsion for heroin—methadone. That is because methadone does not, cannot, assuage the underlying anguish for which drugs like heroin and cocaine are the desperate remedy.

A *Time* magazine article entitled "Addiction: How We Get Hooked" asked: "Why do some people fall so easily into the thrall of alcohol, cocaine, nicotine and other addictive substances?" The answer, it said, "may be simpler than anyone dared imagine": dopamine, "the master molecule of addiction . . . As scientists learn more about how dopamine works, the evidence suggests that we may be fighting the wrong battle [in the war on drugs]." Among the persons quoted is Nora Volkow, a PET expert at Brookhaven Laboratories, who says, "Addiction . . . is a disorder of the brain no different from other forms of mental illness." That new insight, *Time* intones, may be the "most important contribution" of the dopamine hypothesis to the fight against drugs.

Given the exclusive biological slant and naive enthusiasm of the *Time* article, one is not surprised at its omission of an established fact of enormous clinical relevance: that the course of addictive behavior can be influenced by the very consequences of the drug-taking itself. When the addict reacts to adverse consequences of drug use—economic, health, legal, and personal—by eventually quitting drugs, reducing use, changing his pattern of use, or getting help, he does so voluntarily. Rather than being the inevitable, involuntary product of a diseased brain, these actions represent the essence of voluntariness. The addict's behavior can be modified by knowledge of the consequences. Involuntary behavior cannot.

Clinical Features of Addiction

Addiction as a term does not exist in the formal medical lexicon, but drug addiction is generally equated with "drug dependence." In the American Psychiatric Association's *Diagnostic and Statistical Disorders Manual* (fourth edition), dependence denotes the persistent, compulsive, time-consuming use of a substance despite harmful consequences and often despite an expressed desire not to use it. Most dependent users develop tolerance—they must keep increasing doses to achieve a desired effect. They experience withdrawal symptoms and intense craving when the substance is stopped abruptly, followed by relief when use is resumed.

It is common for heroin-dependent persons to lose the ability to feel euphoric from the drug, yet continue to seek it solely to keep from going into withdrawal ("getting sick"). Withdrawal from heroin (and other opiate drugs including Demerol, morphine, Percocet, and codeine) or from alcohol, but not from cocaine, causes a predictable pattern of physical symptoms. Recall Jack Lemmon in the movie *Days of Wine and Roses*, sweating, anxious, his body racked with tremors, desperate for alcohol after running out of whiskey. Or Frank Sinatra in *Man With the Golden Arm*, the heroin addict suffering painful muscle cramps and powerful cravings for heroin after his last fix wears off.

Unlike heroin and alcohol, cocaine does not produce such physical withdrawal symptoms. The heavy cocaine addict typically uses the drug (by inhalation or injection) in a driven, repetitive manner for 24 to 72 hours straight. Cocaine wears off very quickly, and as it fades the yearning for more is overpowering. Each fresh hit quells the intense craving. The process winds down when the addict becomes too exhausted, runs out of money, or becomes too paranoid, a potential effect of cocaine and other stimulants, such as methamphetamine. He then "crashes" into a phase of agitated depression and hunger, followed by sleep for 12 to 36 hours. Within hours to days after awakening he experiences powerful urges to use, and the cycle resumes.

Holding Addicts Responsible

To characterize addiction as a disease is not necessarily morally incompatible with saying that addicts are responsible for yielding to it. This is admittedly a demanding approach to responsibility, but our criminal law has always set the bar pretty high. Holding addicts responsible is also strongly supported on utilitarian grounds because the threat of sanctions provides leverage to press them into treatment. Such a stern approach may be thought to be both unfair and unduly paternalistic. However, focusing on relapse suggests a more gentle, less jarring way of thinking about the addict's responsibility: after detoxification and acute treatment, the addict is responsible for taking steps to manage his or her addiction.

In this connection, the similarity between addiction and other chronic diseases, which lies at the heart of the brain disease claim, is particularly important. Yes, addiction is best understood as a chronic relapsing disorder. This helps to establish realistic expectations for the benefits of treatment. But it also emphasizes the important role of behavior in disease management and points in the direction of a theory of responsibility for managing one's own illness.

Richard J. Bonnie, *Social Research*, Fall 2001.

It is almost impossible for a regular user in the midst of a cocaine binge or experiencing the withdrawal of heroin to stop using the drugs if they are available. He is presumably in the "brain disease" state, when use is most compulsive, neuronal disruption most intense. True, purposeful behavior can occur even in this state—for example, the attempt, sometimes violent, to get money or drugs is highly goal-directed—but at the same time the phase can be so urgent and impossible to derail that addicts ignore their screaming babies, frantically gouge themselves with dirty needles, and ruin families, careers, and reputations.

Choosing to End an Addiction

Nonetheless, most addicts have broken the cycle many times. Either they decide to go "cold turkey" or they end up doing so, unintentionally, by running out of drugs or money or landing in jail. Some heroin addicts admit themselves to the hospital to detoxify because they want to quit; others do so to reduce the cost of their habit, knowing they'll be more sensitive to the effects of heroin afterward. The latter behavior, while motivated by an effort to use drugs more efficiently, is nonetheless a purposeful step that the addict could have taken to reexert lasting control.

In the days between binges cocaine addicts make many deliberate choices, and one of those choices could be the choice to stop using the drug. Heroin-dependent individuals, by comparison, use the drug several times a day but can be quite functional in all respects as long as they have stable access to some form of opiate drug in order to prevent withdrawal symptoms. Certainly some addicts may "nod off" in abandoned buildings, true to stereotype, if they consume more opiate than the amount to which their bodies have developed tolerance, but others can be "actively engaged in activities and relationships," according to the ethnographers Edward Preble and John J. Casey Jr.: "The brief moments of euphoria after each administration constitute a small fraction of their daily lives. The rest of the time they are aggressively pursuing a career . . . hustling."

Not always hustling, however. According to the Office of National Drug Control Policy, as many as 46 percent of drug users not in treatment report legal-only sources of income, and 42 percent report both legal and illegal. The National Institute of Justice found that 33–67 percent of arrested drug users indicate "full and part time work" as their main source of income. These surveys do not relate income source to severity of addiction, and it is reasonable to assume that the heaviest users participate least in the legitimate economy. Nonetheless, the fact that many committed drug users do have jobs shows that addiction does not necessarily preclude deliberate, planned activity. . . .

Labeling addiction a chronic and relapsing brain disease succeeds more as sloganism than as public health education.

By locating addiction in the brain, not the person, NIDA has generated an unwarranted level of enthusiasm about pharmacology for drug addiction. By down-playing the volitional dimension of addiction, the brain-disease model detracts from the great promise of strategies and therapies that rely on sanctions and rewards to shape self-control. And by reinforcing a dichotomy between punitive and clinical approaches to addiction, the model devalues the enormous contribution of criminal justice to combating addiction.

The fact that many, perhaps most, addicts are in control of their actions and appetites for circumscribed periods of time shows that they are not perpetually helpless victims of a chronic disease. They are instigators of their addiction, just as they are agents of their own recovery . . . or nonrecovery. The potential for self-control should allow society to endorse expectations and demands of addicts that would never be made of someone with a true involuntary illness. Making such demands is, of course, no assurance that they'll be met. But confidence in their very legitimacy would encourage a range of policy and therapeutic options—using consequences and coercion—that is incompatible with the idea of a no-fault brain disease.

Efforts to neutralize the stigma of addiction by convincing the public that the addict has a "brain disease" are understandable, but in the long run they have no more likelihood of success than the use of feel-good slogans to help a child acquire "self-esteem." Neither respectability nor a sense of self-worth can be bestowed; both must be earned. The best way for any institution, politician, or advocate to combat the stigma of addiction is to promote conditions— both within treatment settings and in society at large—that help the addict develop self-discipline and, along with it, self-respect. In this way, former addicts become visible symbols of hard work, responsibility, and lawfulness—potent antidotes to stigma.

This prescription does not deny whatever biological or psychological vulnerabilities individuals may have. Instead, it makes their struggle to master themselves all the more ennobling.

"We might find the root cause of addiction in our genetic makeup."

Some Chemical Dependency Is Caused by Genetic Factors

Ernest P. Noble

In the following viewpoint, Ernest P. Noble argues that some people may have a genetic propensity for drug addiction. According to Noble, people with a particular variation of what researchers have nicknamed the "pleasure-seeking" gene may turn to drugs to increase their brains' dopamine levels. He asserts that by understanding the nature of this genetic variation, more innovative treatment options can be developed. Noble is a professor of psychiatry and the director of the Alcohol Research Center at UCLA's Neuropsychiatric Institute and Hospital.

As you read, consider the following questions:
1. According to Noble, what percentage of American adults is addicted?
2. In Noble's opinion, which therapies will best help drug abusers who are genetically predisposed to addiction?

Ernest P. Noble, "Addiction May Be in the Genes," *Los Angeles Times*, December 4, 2000. Copyright © 2000 by *Los Angeles Times*. Reproduced by permission.

Why would a talented and successful actor like Robert Downey Jr. repeatedly risk his career for the sake of a drug-induced high?

For many addicts like Downey, the answer may lie not in their upbringing or the company they keep, but in their genetic makeup.

A Changing View of Addiction

And for drug users whose DNA plays a role in their habit, clinicians need to turn their attention to new treatment options that address the genetics of addiction.

Downey's very public yet personal struggle is a familiar story to millions of Americans who struggle with addiction. A quarter of the U.S. adult population is hooked on alcohol, cocaine, nicotine, amphetamines or some other substance.

Through most of the 20th century, we viewed addiction largely as the product of a flawed upbringing or bad character. Addicts deserved punishment, not sympathy.

Studies comparing the lifestyles and habits of twins and adopted children first suggested that addictive behavior has a hereditary component. We began to consider the possibility that we might find the root cause of addiction in our genetic makeup. A major breakthrough in understanding the genetics of addiction came in 1990, when researchers first linked a gene called DRD2—later nicknamed the "pleasure-seeking" gene—to severe alcoholism.

UCLA studies of brain tissue showed that individuals with the "A1 variation" of the DRD2 gene have significantly fewer dopamine receptors in pleasure centers of the brain.

An Addictive Gene

The findings suggest that many addicts use drugs, which increase brain dopamine levels, to compensate for the deficiency in their neurological pleasure system.

Subsequent studies linked the A1 variation of the DRD2 gene to cocaine, amphetamine, heroin and nicotine addiction.

What does this all mean? It means simply that people with this genetic trait are much more susceptible to addiction. In addition, they are more likely to fall prey to the most severe forms of addiction. In fact, data show that while only 10% of the general population in the United States has the A1 variation of the DRD2 gene, it is found in about half of addicts.

Rethinking Treatment Programs

Meanwhile, the implications for treatment programs are becoming increasingly clear. A UCLA study of heroin addicts published [in summer 2000] showed that a high percentage of heroin users who respond poorly to traditional addiction treatment programs have the troublesome A1 variation of the DRD2 gene.

The Genetic Basis of Marijuana Use

Given that marijuana is the Nation's most commonly abused illicit drug, understanding its mechanism of action will be a critical step in developing new therapies for preventing and treating marijuana use. For example, researchers now know that genetic factors may play a larger role than originally thought in how an individual responds to a drug such as marijuana.

Investigators have now determined that heredity strongly influences whether an individual has positive or negative sensations after smoking marijuana. This study demonstrated that identical male twins were more likely than nonidentical male twins to report similar responses to marijuana use, indicating a genetic basis for their sensations. The finding that genetic factors contribute to how an individual feels after using marijuana opens new avenues for prevention and treatment research; it further emphasizes that drug use and addiction are not simply social problems but are health issues affected by an individual's biological state. Environmental factors may lead to an individual's experimenting with a drug, but heredity appears to hold a key to whether an individual will continue to use or abuse the drug.

National Institute on Drug Abuse, *Sixth Triennial Report to Congress*, 2001.

And a study of alcoholics showed that patients with the same "pleasure-seeking" trait responded well to treatment with a nonaddictive drug that stimulates the dopamine receptors.

These findings demand that clinicians rethink treatment options for the millions of drug-users who are genetically predisposed to addiction.

The implications carry additional weight in California, where voter-approved Proposition 36 will divert tens of thousands of addicts a year from the criminal justice system into treatment.

Mitigating the Effects of Addiction

A simple cheek cell test of DNA can help differentiate hard-core, genetic addicts from those who developed bad habits while socializing with bad crowds.

Drug abusers with a genetic propensity toward addiction typically require one of a growing number of innovative prescription drug therapies to beat their habit. Those without the gene more often respond best to counseling that addresses environmental factors that led to their drug abuse.

The more we know about why the body craves drugs and the more we put that knowledge to use, the more successful we will be in mitigating the heavy toll that drug addiction takes on individuals, families and our society.

"Heavy alcohol and drug use appears related to an accumulation of risk factors."

A Variety of Factors Causes Adolescent Drug Abuse

Susan M. Gordon

Teenage drug abuse can be traced to several risk factors, Susan M. Gordon asserts in the following viewpoint. According to Gordon, these factors include teenagers' psychological and genetic makeup, their performance at school, and their level of spirituality. In addition, Gordon argues, adolescents whose families and peers use drugs and alcohol are more likely to become addicted. She concludes that these factors are interconnected and that such interconnections can complicate prevention and treatment efforts. Gordon is the director of research and professional training at the Caron Foundation, an organization dedicated to providing a caring and enlightened treatment community.

As you read, consider the following questions:

1. What are some of the psychological symptoms associated with substance abuse, according to the author?
2. Which theories have been offered to explain why drug abuse may be a family problem?
3. According to Gordon, how does popular culture affect adolescents' views of drugs and alcohol?

Susan M. Gordon, *Adolescent Drug Use: Trends in Abuse, Treatment, and Prevention.* Wernersville, PA: Caron Foundation, 2000. Copyright © 2000 by the Caron Foundation. Reproduced by permission.

Extensive research has identified a wide variety of risk factors that predict adolescent drug use. These risk factors can be separated into individual, social and cultural factors. Not all children or adolescents who experience these risk factors will use or abuse drugs. Heavy alcohol and drug use appears related to an accumulation of risk factors. Identifying young people who experience a constellation of risk factors can increase the possibility of early intervention before addiction occurs.

Individual risk factors pertain to a person's psychological make-up and symptoms, perceptions about the danger of drugs, behavior and spirituality.

Psychological and Genetic Links

Psychological and genetic links to substance abuse include a genetic predisposition to alcoholism and addictive disorders. Studies involving adopted children and identical twins point to high relationships between genetic factors and the transmission of alcoholism.

Developmental disorders, such as attention deficit hyperactivity disorder and learning disabilities, also may predispose a person to drug or alcohol abuse. More than one-quarter of adolescents in treatment at the Caron Foundation have been diagnosed with a learning disability or reported experiencing symptoms of a learning disability.

Psychological symptoms, such as depression, impulsivity and emotional unsteadiness, may also increase vulnerability to substance abuse. Also, young people who use marijuana to alleviate psychological symptoms are less likely to stop its use than youths who use it for social reasons.

Gender Differences

Male adolescents are more likely to have a combination of conduct disorders and substance abuse, while female adolescents have coexisting affective disorders and substance abuse. In addition, girls are more susceptible to substance abuse if they have an eating disorder, such as bulimia or anorexia, or if they have experienced early onset of puberty. [Carlos M.] Grillo and his colleagues examined gender differences on an adolescent psychiatric unit and discovered that the girls were more likely to have oppositional defiant disorder, eating disorders, borderline personality disorder and polysubstance disorders in addition to alcohol abuse.

There also appears to be gender differences between the types of trauma to which children and adolescents are exposed. Adolescent boys in treatment for drug and alcohol problems are more likely than girls to report histories of physical abuse. Likewise, adolescent girls in treatment are more likely than boys to report histories of sexual abuse. Childhood sexual abuse appears to be a predictor of substance abuse and dependence among adult women. Research studies that question adults about childhood trauma find that women with histories of childhood sexual abuse are much more likely to report drug and alcohol problems than women without histories of childhood sexual abuse.

Behavioral Risk Factors

Behavioral risk factors include poor school performance, violence and delinquency and sexual promiscuity. Adolescents who do not achieve good grades or who view themselves as poor students are at risk for substance abuse. Likewise, school dropouts are more likely to abuse drugs and alcohol than those who remain in school. In addition, school dropouts are less likely than graduates to stop using drugs in adulthood.

Teenagers who break the law through behaviors, such as fighting and carrying weapons, are also at risk for substance abuse. In 1993, of the adolescents in New York City who had been in juvenile custody, 60 percent also had abused and/or sold drugs and alcohol. Also, adolescents who use alcohol and marijuana are more likely than other teenagers to be sexually active and not use protective devices, leading to unwanted pregnancies and sexually transmitted diseases.

Spirituality

The lack of expression of spirituality through religious attendance also appears to be a risk factor for drug use. The less frequently an adolescent attends religious services, the more likely it is that the adolescent will smoke, drink or use marijuana. In their investigation of the initiation factors to marijuana use, [Denise B.] Kandel and [Mark] Davies found that frequent attendance at religious services decreases the risk of drug use. It is interesting that almost half of the adolescents who come into substance abuse treatment at the Caron Foundation list "none" for their religious preference.

Families Are a Major Influence

Social risk factors involve the environments in which children and adolescents spend most of their time and which have the greatest influence over the child's development: family, peers, community and youth culture.

Family involvement can be a major force influencing recovery. Although most parents attempt to do their best, no family is perfect and poor family functioning can become a risk factor for drug abuse. Aspects of family functioning that have a negative effect on adolescent development are family tolerance of substance use and abuse; inadequate parental guidance; and family conflict and poor bonding.

Thompson. © 2001 by Copley Media Services. Reprinted with permission.

The lack of parental presence is an important risk factor for adolescents. Adolescents who do not find a parent at home after school are more likely to smoke tobacco regularly, drink and get drunk regularly and use marijuana. Unsupervised adolescents report greater interest in trying other illegal drugs in the future than teenagers who have a parent at home after school. The more often parents eat with their children, the less likely it is that their children will smoke, drink or use other drugs.

Kandel and Davies also found a relationship between adolescent marijuana use and parental use of medically prescribed psychotropic drugs. They also found that adolescents who progress to regular marijuana use are more likely to have a family history of psychological or substance abuse problems. It appears that substance abuse may be a family problem because often more than one family member will abuse or be dependent upon drugs or alcohol. However, the causes for family use are not clear. Theories range from genetic effects in which predisposition to substance abuse is biologically passed to family members, to social modeling theories which posit that behaviors are learned from observation.

High levels of family conflict and poor bonding also are associated with substance abuse among the young. Childhood sexual and/or physical abuse often is a precursor to adolescent and adult substance abuse for both males and females. Almost 40 percent of adolescents who come to the Caron Foundation for treatment have histories of either physical and/or sexual abuse.

Peer Influences

Youths exist in systems larger than their families. They go to school, hold part-time jobs and interact in a wide variety of ways with the larger community. Peers play important roles in recovery and are major influences in the risk for drug use. Adolescents surveyed in Pennsylvania reported they were most likely to use drugs or alcohol at parties, at their friends' homes or at home.

Peer involvement with substance abuse becomes a powerful predictor for relapse. Among the adolescents who attended inpatient treatment at the Caron Foundation, we found that the greater the extent of substance use among a teenager's friends, the lower the likelihood that the teenager would be able to maintain abstinence following treatment.

Often the way teenagers think about their friends can influence their susceptibility to substance abuse. If adolescents overestimate substance use among their friends, they will be more likely to abuse drugs and alcohol. Adolescent girls may be more vulnerable than boys to peer pressure since their initiation to marijuana use has been related to the number of friends who used the drug.

Other Risk Factors

It is important not to neglect the risk factors for drug use in the larger environment of the adolescent. Neighborhoods in which children are exposed to drug use or where people do not look out for each other's children increase a child's risk for substance abuse. Although drugs are more easily found in poor areas, disconnected communities exist in all socioeconomic levels.

Of course, the influence of popular culture cannot be underestimated. Images on television, in the movies, music and magazines, as well as on the Internet often glamorize the use of drugs and alcohol. A survey of the 200 most popular movie rentals from 1996 and 1997 found more than 90 percent of the movies showed alcohol and tobacco use and 22 percent of the movies depicted illegal drug use, although less than half of the films showed consequences of substance use. Children and adolescents may become seduced by these media into thinking that drugs and alcohol are not dangerous, but fun. (CASA) found that organizations such as the Partnership for a Drug-Free America that advertise anti-drug messages have difficulty getting broadcast time on television stations.

Although we can separate risk factors into separate categories, it is important to remember that one risk factor in one category does not automatically result in drug abuse. For example, a genetic predisposition to alcohol dependence will result in alcoholism only when the individual lives in an environment that encourages drinking. As a different example, a dysfunctional family relationship that results in physical or sexual abuse may trigger other risk factors, such as depression and posttraumatic stress syndrome, which together increase one's vulnerability to substance abuse.

Likewise, [Helen E.] Garnier and her colleagues found interconnecting links to drug use, school performance and family values. Exposure to drugs in childhood increases the risk for adolescent drug use and increased stressful life events. Drug use and stressful life events are both related to poor school performance that can result in the student dropping out, increasing the risk for continued drug abuse.

No one lives in a vacuum. The interconnections of factors leading to risk for substance abuse highlight the interconnections in human development among the person, society and culture. These interconnections complicate treatment and prevention efforts because more than one factor must be addressed. However, the interconnections also provide multiple openings for treatment and prevention programs.

"Few movies emphasized the illegal nature of drug use; only 28 percent associated illicit drugs with crime or violence."

Movies Present Mixed Messages About Substance Abuse

Office of National Drug Control Policy and Substance Abuse and Mental Health Services Administration

In the following viewpoint, the Office of National Drug Control Policy (ONDCP) and the Substance Abuse and Mental Health Services Administration (SAMHSA) contend that movies often present substance abuse in a positive light, including the portrayal of drug use, smoking, and drinking among adolescent characters. Although substance abuse is sometimes associated with negative consequences, such as crime, the authors assert that movies frequently link drug use to wealth and humorous situations. ONDCP formulates the government's national drug strategy. SAMHSA is aimed at improving the quality of prevention, treatment, and rehabilitative services.

As you read, consider the following questions:
1. Illicit drugs appear in what percentage of movies, according to the study?
2. According to the authors, how many movies contained negative statements about drug use?
3. How was adolescent drug use typically portrayed, in the authors' views?

Office of National Drug Control Policy and Substance Abuse and Mental Health Services Administration, *Substance Abuse in Popular Movies and Music*, April 1999.

How do movies depict substance use?

The Frequency of Substance Use

Few movies were "substance free;" only 5 of the 200 movies portrayed no substance use whatsoever (about 2 percent). Illicit drugs appeared in 22 percent of the movies, tobacco in 89 percent, alcohol in 93 percent, and other legal drugs (prescription or over-the-counter medicines) in 29 percent.

Movies were rarely about substance use. Use constituted an important theme in only 6 percent of the movies.

One or more major characters used illicit drugs in 12 percent of the movies, tobacco in 44 percent, and alcohol in 85 percent.

Some movies (15 percent) portrayed substance use by characters who appeared to be younger than 18 years old. These characters used illicit drugs in 3 percent of the movies, tobacco in 8 percent, and alcohol in 9 percent.

Negative statements about substance use (advocating abstinence or criticizing drinking, smoking, or drug use) occurred in 31 percent of the movies. Eleven percent contained statements about limits on how much, how often, where, or when substances were consumed; most of these comments referred to tobacco.

Positive statements about substance use (e.g., expressing longing, desire, or favorable attributes of use) occurred in 29 percent of all movies. Most pro-use statements referred to alcohol. About half (49 percent) of all movies depicted one or more short-term consequences of substance use.

Only 7 percent of movies depicted long-term consequences; an additional 5 percent included dialogue from which long-term consequences could be inferred (e.g., references to alcoholism or to characters who overdosed). . . .

How Frequently Do Substances Appear Within Movies?

In order to compare substance use in movies of different lengths, the movies were first divided into 5-minute intervals, yielding a total of 4,372 intervals. The presence or absence of each substance was recorded for every interval. The proportion of intervals in which each substance appeared was then calculated.

Illicit drugs appeared infrequently—in 2 percent of all intervals.

Tobacco appeared in 24 percent.

Alcohol appeared in 31 percent.

Other legal drugs appeared in 3 percent. . . .

How Common Is Substance Use Among Major Characters?

This section describes the prevalence of substance use—that is, the proportion of major characters that used illicit drugs, tobacco, alcohol, or other substances (such as prescription or over-the-counter medicines). The results are presented separately for adult and young characters.

Substance Abuse Among Adults

Of the 669 adult major characters, most were male (67 percent), between ages 18 and 39 (71 percent), and middle class (69 percent).

The majority were white (81 percent), followed by African American (13 percent), Latino (3 percent), Asian (2 percent), and other groups (less than 1 percent). Only 21 percent occupied the role of antagonist or villain; the remainder were coded as protagonists.

Thirty-three adult characters (5 percent) used illicit drugs, 25 percent smoked, 65 percent consumed alcohol, and 5 percent used other substances.

Characters consumed more than one substance (often at the same time): 70 percent who smoked also drank alcohol; 85 percent who used illicit drugs also used tobacco or alcohol.

Few major characters described themselves as having quit or having tried to quit using illicit drugs, alcohol, or tobacco. Five characters described themselves as former drug users and one quit a drug habit during the movie. Five characters described themselves as former drinkers and three as former smokers. One character attempted to quit smoking (and she failed).

More white than African-American characters used illicit drugs in these movies. Although African Americans represented a small portion of all major characters, their proportional illicit drug use was higher (10 percent) than among white characters (5 percent). Use by characters of other ethnic groups was not portrayed.

Gender Roles and Socioeconomic Status

Illicit drug use was more prevalent among characters with low socioeconomic status (18 percent) than middle (4 percent) or high socioeconomic status (5 percent), and more prevalent among adults under 40 than among older adults (6 percent v. 2 percent).

Illicit drug use was unrelated to gender or role; drug users were as likely to be male as female, protagonist as antagonist.

Smoking was more prevalent among men than women (28 percent v. 21 percent) and more prevalent among antagonists than protagonists (38 percent v. 22 percent).

Smoking was more common among characters with low (36 percent) and high socioeconomic status (31 percent) than middle (23 percent) but unrelated to characters' age or ethnicity.

Alcohol consumption was more prevalent among characters with lower (55 percent) and middle socioeconomic status (54 percent) than with high (44 percent). Alcohol use was unrelated to characters' gender, age, ethnicity, or role.

Drinking and smoking "on the job" was not uncommon— 19 percent of characters who used alcohol and 42 percent of those who used tobacco did so at their workplace or while "on duty."

Forty-two percent of major characters who used illicit drugs, 7 percent who smoked, and 16 percent who drank experienced some consequence of their use.

Substance Abuse Among Youth

The 79 major characters who appeared to be under 18 were primarily white (85 percent), middle class (71 percent), and protagonists (92 percent). About half of these young characters were female (47 percent).

Of the characters who appeared to be under 18, 8 percent used illicit drugs, 17 percent smoked, 22 percent drank alcohol, and 4 percent used other substances.

Of six major characters in this age group who used illicit drugs, five were seen smoking marijuana and one claimed to have used crack.

Of the young characters who smoked, 39 percent also drank alcohol. Smoking was slightly more common among girls than boys (19 percent vs. 14 percent); other substance use was unrelated to gender.

None of the young characters who smoked marijuana or cigarettes experienced any apparent consequences of their use.

Forty percent of the young characters who consumed alcohol experienced one or more consequences from drinking.

How Do Movies Portray Illicit Drug Use?

Percentages are based on 43 movies in which illicit drugs appeared or 67 scenes that portrayed illicit drug use by any character.

The appearance of illicit drugs was not always synonymous with use.

Characters used illicit drugs in 77 percent of the movies in which illicit drugs appeared.

Marijuana was found more frequently (51 percent) than any other illegal drug, followed by powdered cocaine (33 percent). Heroin, crack cocaine, and other illicit drugs appeared infrequently.

Few movies emphasized the illegal nature of drug use; only 28 percent associated illicit drugs with crime or violence.

About one-fourth (26 percent) of the movies contained explicit, graphic portrayals of preparing and/or using illicit drugs. About one-fourth (23 percent) showed characters refusing specific invitations to use.

Twenty-six percent portrayed illicit drug use in humorous contexts, 16 percent at parties, and 12 percent in wealthy, luxurious settings.

Five movies contained negative statements (advocating abstinence or criticizing illicit drug use) and five contained positive statements about drug use.

Marijuana use was portrayed most frequently (in 57 percent of the scenes), followed by heroin or other opiates (18 percent), and powder cocaine (13 percent). The remaining

12 percent of scenes involved a variety of other illicit substances, including crank, crack, LSD, and PCP.

Most of the scenes (69 percent) showed illicit drug use by at least one major character.

Reasons for Illicit Drug Use

Most scenes (72 percent) portrayed no clear motive for illicit drug use. When a motive was evident, addiction was the reason in 10 percent of the scenes, stress relief or mood management in another 10 percent, and circumstances of the plot in the remaining 8 percent of the scenes.

Few scenes (17 percent) showed people using illicit drugs while alone. Most portrayals emphasized the social nature of illicit drug use, more often showing drug use by groups of two or three characters in private rather than at gatherings such as parties or other celebrations.

Some scenes associated illicit drug use with risk-taking activities such as crime or violence (22 percent) and driving a car (11 percent). Sexual activity was associated with illicit drug use in 9 percent of the scenes.

One or more consequences of illicit drug use were portrayed in 34 percent of the scenes, typically showing how drug use alters a character's physical or mental state.

Few scenes emphasized the illegal nature of illicit drug use; the legal consequences of use (arrest or conviction) were rarely portrayed.

How Are Alcohol and Tobacco Portrayed on Screen?

Percentages are based on 183 movies that depicted alcohol use or 172 movies that portrayed tobacco use.

Characters drank hard liquor or mixed drinks in 78 percent of the movies, wine or champagne in 78 percent, and beer in 66 percent.

More movies expressed positive statements about drinking alcohol (20 percent) than negative statements (9 percent). In addition, few movies (14 percent) showed characters who refused a drink, and only 6 percent explicitly advocated limits on where, when, or how much alcohol should be consumed.

Alcohol consumption was frequently portrayed in positive contexts. About half of the movies depicted alcohol use at parties (49 percent), 24 percent associated its use with humor, and 34 percent with images of wealth.

Drinking alcohol was frequently associated with taking risks—crime or violence in 38 percent of the movies, driving a car in 14 percent, and other risky behaviors in 7 percent. It was associated with sexual activity in 19 percent.

Types of Illicit Drugs, Tobacco, and Alcohol in Movies

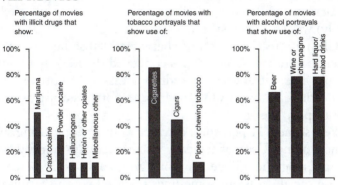

Percentage of movies with illicit drugs that show:

Percentage of movies with tobacco portrayals that show use of:

Percentage of movies with alcohol portrayals that show use of:

Based on 43 movies in which illicit drugs appeared, 172 movies portraying tobacco use, and 183 movies portraying alcohol use. Percentages sum to more than 100% because multiple substances appeared in the same movie.

Office of National Drug Control Policy and Department of Health and Human Services Substance Abuse and Mental Health Services Administration, "Substance Use in Popular Movies and Music," April 1999.

Characters smoked cigarettes in 85 percent of the movies, cigars in 45 percent, and pipes in 10 percent. Characters chewed tobacco in 2 percent.

Positive statements about smoking/smokers occurred infrequently (6 percent). Nearly one-fourth of the movies (22 percent) expressed negative statements about smoking or smokers, but few movies (7 percent) showed characters who refused to smoke.

More movies associated smoking with crime or violence (34 percent) than with images of wealth (18 percent), parties (18 percent), or humor (10 percent). Only 5 percent of movies associated smoking with sex.

How Do Movies Portray Substance Use by Youth?

Percentages are based on all scenes depicting substance use by characters who appeared to be under 18.

Twenty-nine movies (15 percent) portrayed substance use by underage characters in 98 different scenes; about half of these scenes involved a major character who appeared to be under 18.

Most scenes portrayed young characters smoking cigarettes, drinking alcohol, or both. Characters assumed to be under 18 smoked cigarettes in 51 percent of the scenes (a cigar in one scene), and consumed alcohol (mostly beer) in 46 percent of the scenes. Illicit drug use (marijuana exclusively) was shown in six scenes.

Clear motives for young characters' substance use were rarely portrayed. A few scenes conveyed the idea that young people use substances to reduce stress or improve their mood or self-image. Only one scene portrayed use as a result of peer pressure.

Few scenes (11 percent) portrayed young people using substances alone. Use was typically a social activity—mostly boys and girls together (59 percent) or a group of boys (35 percent). These social occasions sometimes involved youth sharing the same drink or smoking the same cigarette or joint (16 percent).

Young characters either drank alcohol (beer or hard liquor) or smoked (cigarettes or marijuana) at school in 13 percent of these scenes.

No scenes showed young characters using alcohol or illicit drugs in a car, but a few scenes associated substance use with sex or other adolescent high-risk behaviors.

Young characters rarely experienced any consequences of substance use. Only 13 percent of scenes portrayed any consequences, and only 10 percent depicted any consequences to a major character. The instances in which consequences were shown involved physical reactions to drinking alcohol, smoking cigarettes, or marijuana (such as loss of motor control, slurred speech, headaches, or coughing). . . .

The Power of the Media

This study examines the frequency and nature of substance use in the most popular movie rentals . . . of 1996 and 1997.

The intent was to determine the accuracy of public perceptions about extensive substance use in media popular among youth. Because teenagers are major consumers of movies . . . there is concern about the potential for media depictions of tobacco, alcohol, and illicit drugs to encourage use. For instance, portrayals that tend to legitimize, normalize, trivialize, or glorify substances might suggest to young people that this behavior is without negative consequences. Careful examination of media content is a crucial first step in determining what role media may play in promoting substance use and abuse.

Periodical Bibliography

The following articles have been selected to supplement the diverse views presented in this chapter.

Melissa Abramovitz	"Addiction," *Current Health 2*, September 1999.
Scott Baldauf	"When Parents Are a Part of the Drug Problem," *Christian Science Monitor*, August 28, 2000.
Janet Kay Bobo and Corinne Husten	"Sociocultural Influences on Smoking and Drinking," *Alcohol Research & Health*, Winter 2000.
Richard J. Bonnie	"Addiction and Responsibility," *Social Research*, Fall 2001.
Joseph A. Califano Jr.	"It's All in the Family," *America*, January 15, 2000.
Joseph A. Califano Jr.	"The Grass Roots of Teen Drug Abuse," *Wall Street Journal*, March 26, 1999.
Siobhan Gorman	"Why They Don't Just Say No," *National Journal*, August 18, 2001.
Harvard Mental Health Letter	"Addiction and the Brain—Part II," July 1998.
Constance Holden	"New Clues to Alcoholism Risk," *Science*, May 29, 1998.
Norbert R. Myslinski	"Addiction's Ugly Face," *World & I*, December 1999.
Tabitha M. Powledge	"Addiction and the Brain," *BioScience*, July 1999.
Sally Satel	"Drugs: A Decision, Not a Disease," *Wall Street Journal*, April 27, 2001.
Joshua Wolf Shenk	"America's Altered States," *Harper's Magazine*, May 1999.

CHAPTER 3

What Drug Treatment and Prevention Programs Are Effective?

Chapter Preface

One of the curiosities about drug addiction is that addicts can often be cured of their dependency by taking other drugs. Methadone is probably the best known of these substitute drugs, but another drug, ibogaine, has shown promise as a treatment in recent years.

Ibogaine began to be developed as a treatment for chemical dependency in the early 1960s. Traditionally used as a hallucinogen in Africa, ibogaine is derived from the plant *Tabernanthe iboga*. Its effectiveness in treating addiction—both heroin and cocaine—was discovered in 1962 by Howard Lotsof. The National Institute on Drug Abuse and drug rehabilitation centers in New York, the Netherlands, and Panama have since conducted studies on the drug's efficacy. Tests have shown that ibogaine is 70 percent effective in treating chemical dependency and is not addictive. Nearly 25 percent of addicts who received ibogaine treatment in Europe remained drug-free for at least six months, while another 45 percent successfully combined ibogaine with other treatments.

Addicts are typically given dosages of ibogaine ranging from fifteen to twenty-five milligrams over a two-day period. Researchers say that the drug works by reducing the supply of dopamine to the brain, hastening withdrawal, while at the same time increasing the brain's supply of serotonin, which eases often-painful withdrawal symptoms. Another theory points to the psychoactive effects of the hallucinogen. According to Lotsof and others, addicts taking ibogaine release and then reevaluate repressed memories, enabling them to understand why they used drugs.

Although ibogaine might seem to be a promising treatment, it has yet to develop a foothold in the United States for several reasons. Of greatest concern are the deaths that have been linked to ibogaine, including a woman who died of a heroin overdose while taking ibogaine, possibly because ibogaine can increase the toxic effects of heroin. The drug has also been linked to seizures and brain damage in rats, and cardiac arrest in dogs. Because of these problems, and because of the hallucinogenic properties of ibogaine, the U.S. Drug Enforcement Agency has defined ibogaine and the plant *Taber-*

nanthe iboga as Schedule 1 drugs, or substances that have "a high potential for abuse [and] no currently accepted medical use in treatment in the United States."

Ibogaine may never become an officially sanctioned treatment for heroin and cocaine addiction in the United States. However, a variety of treatment options, including those that use substitute drugs, are available to addicts. In the following chapter, the authors evaluate the effectiveness of several of these programs.

"If you're so inhumane that you don't care about the addicts themselves, care about their partners and babies, because they are also not getting infected, [because of needle-exchange programs]."

Needle-Exchange Programs Can Reduce the Transmission of AIDS

Peter Beilenson, interviewed by Will Van Sant

In the following viewpoint, Peter Beilenson asserts that needle-exchange programs, in which sterile needles are distributed to heroin addicts, help prevent the transmission of the AIDS virus. According to Beilenson, needle-exchange programs have been especially effective in Baltimore, Maryland, because AIDS cases in that city are caused primarily by intravenous drug users sharing dirty needles. He contends that by reducing the transmission of the virus, the Baltimore program saves the city millions of dollars in health care costs. Beilenson is Baltimore's public health commissioner and Will Van Sant is a journalist.

As you read, consider the following questions:
1. According to Beilenson, what percentage of AIDS cases in Baltimore has been injection-drug users?
2. How much did the first four years of the Baltimore needle-exchange program cost?
3. In Beilenson's opinion, how do needle exchanges affect adolescent drug use?

Peter Beilenson, "On Pins and Needles," *National Journal*, vol. 31, May 15, 1999, p. 1,341. Copyright © 1999 by *National Journal*. Reproduced by permission.

A lthough research shows that needle-exchange programs can save lives and taxpayer dollars, Congress and many states and cities have kept their distance from them. Many lawmakers argue that public money shouldn't be used to make it easier for lawbreaking drug addicts to maintain their habits. "The best way to deal with the addiction is to not use drugs in the first place," ex-Rep. Gerald B.H. Solomon, R-N.Y., said [in April 1998]. "Just like Nancy Reagan used to say when she was here: 'Just say no.'"

Baltimore's Dr. Peter Beilenson, a leading proponent of needle exchanges, has been the city's public health commissioner since 1992. Beilenson and Mayor Kurt L. Schmoke have initiated several controversial health policy changes, including making contraceptives available in public schools. In August 1994, the mayor and his health commissioner established a needle-exchange program, and the success of that program has, over time, made believers of many conservative state legislators. Beilenson spoke with *National Journal* about needle exchanges—and the politicians who oppose them. The following are excerpts from that conversation:

A Lifesaving Policy

Q: *How widespread are these exchanges?*

A: There are over a hundred around the country. About half are illegal. The legal programs are mostly operated by advocacy groups. They typically travel around in vans or set up on a street corner and hand out sterile needles. Our program is the eighth-largest in the country, and it's the largest city-government-run program. It's unusually well structured. Every needle that goes out, we know who took how many. We do HIV screening. We've gotten about a thousand people into treatment.

Q: *Have lives been saved, and infections prevented, by the Baltimore program?*

A: Probably about 500 AIDS cases have been prevented. That's just among our clients. That doesn't count infections that otherwise could have been passed on to babies, spouses, or sex partners. In Baltimore, HIV/AIDS was the No. 1 killer of 25- to 44-year-olds—black, white, male, female—in the early '90s. It still is. Nearly 80 percent of our AIDS cases have been injection-drug users. It's totally not a gay disease in Baltimore. It almost never really has been—it used to be more 50/50 and now it's more 80 [percent injection-drug users]/20 [percent gays]. We're talking a thousand-plus HIV infections a year in Baltimore in the early '90s. This was an epidemic. In '93, there were 1,378 new infections reported. In 1998, that number fell to 544, thanks largely to the availability of clean needles. HIV infection among IV drug users themselves has declined 30 percent since needle exchange started. That's in the city. Meanwhile, it's up 5 percent in Baltimore County, which has no exchange program.

Q: Has your program produced any savings?

A: The average AIDS case used to cost about $120,000 a

Drug Use Behavior That Transmits HIV

Pregnant mothers infected with HIV risk passing the virus to their infants perinatally (sometime around the time of birth). Researchers estimate that a woman has a 13 to 40 percent chance of passing HIV infection to her infant. Moreover, pregnancy itself may accelerate the course of HIV disease in the mother, most likely as a result of an altered immune system during pregnancy.

Very little is known about female IV drug users' contraceptive practices to avoid transmission of HIV. Although heroin can suppress fertility to some degree in women, New York City officials report that birth rates among addicted women are higher than those among nonaddicted women.

Intravenous drug use, promiscuity, and prostitution are all linked with the lack of contraceptive use. The Centers for Disease Control and Prevention (CDC) reports that the majority of women with AIDS are of childbearing age (20 to 44 years), which indicates the likelihood of an increasing population of children with HIV infection.

While investigators often treat sexual behavior and drug use separately, many times they are linked. Female IV drug users may use sex to obtain drugs from partners who are also IV drug users. Women are much more frequently involved in prostitution to fund drug habits than men. What exacerbates the danger to these women is the powerlessness they experience due to their intense need for drugs and severe poverty. Because many men seek out dangerous sexual services from drug-addicted prostitutes, they are at great risk.

Curtis Jackson-Jacobs, *Illegal Drugs: America's Anguish*, 2002.

year. Now with newer, and more expensive, medication, the yearly cost of treatment can reach $190,000 or so. So you multiply that by the number of lives saved, 500. Virtually all those savings are in taxpayer dollars. These are not addicts who have insurance. These are uninsured addicts who, had they become infected, would unquestionably have been given care paid for by taxpayers. These are direct taxpayer costs that were saved. We've tried to be conservative in calculating savings, so we knocked it down to $30 million. By comparison, the cost of the first four years of the needle-exchange program was about $1.2 million. So it's clearly been cost-beneficial.

Responding to Congressional Criticism

Q: How do you respond to such critics as Rep. Solomon?

A: I'm usually the only testifier for the Democrats when federal funding for needle exchanges comes up. I testified before [Rep. J. Dennis] Hastert's subcommittee before he zoomed up to the speakership. His views were essentially the same as Solomon's. What I strongly encourage Members of Congress to do is what our opponents in the Maryland legislature were honest enough to do a few years ago. They made some of the very same comments when a bill came up in 1994—and barely passed—that exempted us from the state drug paraphernalia law so the Baltimore City Public Health Department could run a needle-exchange program within Baltimore City's borders. I invited them to come to the city and see exactly how things actually operate. To their great credit, most of the people who voted against us in 1994 accepted our invitation. They listened to addicts, talked to them, talked to our staff. When the exemption came up for renewal in 1997, for renewal in perpetuity, it passed, 22–0.

The first thing I would say to Rep. Solomon and Speaker Hastert and everybody else I spoke to on Capitol Hill is, "Drive beyond the Capital Beltway, leave your suburban homes and make your way to an inner-city, drug-infested neighborhood where there are serious problems and where we are making serious attempts to deal with them, and where we are clearly getting the results that everybody in the country would want. Come see how this thing works." We are not handing out needles; this is a needle exchange program. It's gotten 2.3 million dirty, used, blood-filled syringes—AIDS-filled syringes, in many cases—out of circulation in Baltimore and gotten 2.3 million sterile needles to people. If you're so inhumane that you don't care about the addicts themselves, care about their partners and babies, because they are also not getting infected, because of programs like ours.

An implication in all of the congressional criticism is that needle exchange is condoning drug use and making it look—especially to kids—like there's nothing wrong with drugs. So [in 1998] I went to our main researcher at the Johns Hopkins University School of Public Health and asked if anybody had ever studied what kids think about needle-exchange programs. He said no. So we found four high schools—over a thousand kids, a very significant statistical size—in four schools, ninth- and 10th-graders—and asked a bunch of questions. What we found was that needle exchanges are, statistically, as likely to encourage drug use as [are] the anti-drug ads of the drug czar. In other words, they don't encourage drug use.

Politics Versus Science

So a good seven or eight years into good science on needle exchanges, it's clear that there is absolutely no excuse for Congress to continue to deny federal support for these programs. It is absolutely not science; it's completely politics.

"[Needle-exchange program] advocates seem steeped in denial about the behavioral roots of the [drug] crisis."

Needle-Exchange Programs Do Not Reduce the Transmission of AIDS

Joe Loconte

Needle-exchange programs have not been proven to reduce the spread of the AIDS virus, Joe Loconte maintains in the following viewpoint. Loconte argues that studies purporting to show the effectiveness of these programs—in which intravenous drug users are given clean needles so that they do not share contaminated needles with other addicts—are flawed and cannot be considered truly scientific. According to Loconte, advocates of needle-exchange programs ignore the moral and behavioral aspects of drug addiction and neglect more effective ways of conquering drug abuse, such as treatment programs. Loconte is a writer and researcher for the Heritage Foundation's Center for Religion in a Civil Society.

As you read, consider the following questions:
1. What does Loconte label a "profoundly misguided notion"?
2. According to the author, how was the New Haven study on needle-exchange programs flawed?
3. In Loconte's opinion, how would a "truly scientific trial" of needle-exchange programs be conducted?

Joe Loconte, "Killing Them Softly," *Policy Review*, July/August 1998, pp. 14–16. Copyright © 1998 by *Policy Review*. Reproduced by permission.

In a midrise office building on Manhattan's West 37th Street, about two blocks south of the Port Authority bus terminal, sits the Positive Health Project, one of 11 needle-exchange outlets in New York City. This particular neighborhood, dotted by X-rated video stores, peep shows, and a grimy hot dog stand, could probably tolerate some positive health. But it's not clear that's what the program's patrons are getting.

The clients are intravenous (IV) drug users. They swap their used needles for clean ones and, it is hoped, avoid the AIDS virus, at least until their next visit. There's no charge, no hassles, no meddlesome questions. That's just the way Walter, a veteran heroin user, likes it.

"Just put me on an island and don't mess with me," he says, lighting up a cigarette.

A tall, thinnish man, Walter seems weary for his 40-some years. Like many of the estimated 250,000 IV drug users in this city, he has spent years shooting up and has bounced in and out of detoxification programs. "Don't get the idea in your mind you're going to control it," he says. "I thought I could control it. But dope's a different thing. You just want it." Can he imagine his life without drugs? "I'm past that," he says, his face tightening. "The only good thing I do is getting high."

Encouraging Addiction

Supporters of needle-exchange programs (NEPs), from AIDS activists to [former] Secretary of Health and Human Services Donna Shalala, seem to have reached the same verdict on Walter's life. They take his drug addiction as a given, but want to keep him free of HIV by making sure he isn't borrowing dirty syringes. Says Shalala, "This is another life-saving intervention." That message is gaining currency, thanks in part to at least 112 programs in 29 states, distributing millions of syringes each year.

Critics say free needles just make it easier for addicts to go about their business: abusing drugs. Ronn Constable, a Brooklynite who used heroin and cocaine for nearly 20 years, says he would have welcomed the needle-exchange program—for saving him money. "An addict doesn't want to spend a dollar on anything else but his drugs," he says. Do needle exchanges, then, save lives or fuel addiction? The issue flared up [in 1998] when Shalala indicated the Bill Clinton administration would lift the ban on federal funding. Barry McCaffrey, the [former] national drug policy chief, denounced the move, saying it would sanction drug use. Fearing a political debacle, the White House upheld the federal ban but continues to trumpet the effectiveness of NEPs. Meanwhile, Representative Gerald Solomon and Senator Paul Coverdell are pushing legislation in Congress to extend the prohibition indefinitely. [That legislation passed in the House in April 1998 but no further action was taken.]

There is more than politics at work here. The debate reveals a deepening philosophical rift between the medical and moral approaches to coping with social ills.

A Misguided Approach

Joined by much of the scientific community, the Clinton administration has tacitly embraced a profoundly misguided notion: that we must not confront drug abusers on moral or religious grounds. Instead, we should use medical interventions to minimize the harm their behavior invites. Directors of needle-exchange outlets pride themselves on running "nonjudgmental" programs. While insisting they do not encourage illegal drug use, suppliers distribute "safe crack kits" explaining the best ways to inject crack cocaine. Willie Easterlins, an outreach worker at a needle-stocked van in Brooklyn, sums up the philosophy this way: "I have to give you a needle. I can't judge," he says. "That's the first thing they teach us."

This approach, however well intentioned, ignores the soul-controlling darkness of addiction and the moral freefall that sustains it. "When addicts talk about enslavement, they're not exaggerating," says Terry Horton, the medical director of Phoenix House, one of the nation's largest residential treatment centers. "It is their first and foremost priority. Heroin first, then breathing, then food."

It is true that needle-sharing among IV drug users is a major source of HIV transmission, and that the incidence of HIV is rising most rapidly among this group—a population of more than a million people. [In 1997], about 30 percent of all new HIV infections were linked to IV drug use. The Clinton administration is correct to call this a major public-health risk.

Nevertheless, NEP advocates seem steeped in denial about the behavioral roots of the crisis, conduct left unchallenged by easy access to clean syringes. Most IV drug users, in fact, die not from HIV-tainted needles but from other health problems, overdoses, or homicide. By evading issues of personal responsibility, the White House and its NEP allies are neglecting the most effective help for drug abusers: enrollment in tough-minded treatment programs enforced by drug courts. Moreover, in the name of "saving lives," they seem prepared to surrender countless addicts to life on the margins—an existence of scheming, scamming, disease, and premature death.

Science Does Not Support NEPs

[Since 1990], NEPs have secured funding from local departments of public health to establish outlets in 71 cities. But that may be as far as their political argument will take them: Federal law prohibits federal money from flowing to the programs until it can be proved they prevent AIDS without encouraging drug use.

It's no surprise, then, that advocates are trying to enlist science as an ally. They claim that numerous studies of NEPs prove they are effective. Says Sandra Thurman, the [former] director of the Office of National AIDS Policy, "There is very little doubt that these programs reduce HIV transmission." In arguing for federal funding, a White House panel on AIDS cited "clear scientific evidence of the efficacy of such programs."

The studies, though suggestive, prove no such thing. Activists tout the results of a New Haven study, published in the *American Journal of Medicine*, saying the program reduces HIV among participants by a third. Not exactly. Researchers tested needles from anonymous users—not the addicts themselves—to see if they contained HIV. They never measured "seroconversion rates," the portion of participants who became HIV positive during the study. Even Peter

Lurie, a University of Michigan researcher and avid NEP advocate, admits that "the validity of testing of syringes is limited." A likely explanation for the decreased presence of HIV in syringes, according to scientists, is sampling error.

Contamination Continues

In the July 1997 issue of the journal *AIDS*, Canadian researchers reported results from an 18-month study of intravenous drug users in Vancouver [British Columbia, Canada]. That city has the largest needle-exchange program in the Western Hemisphere—and for most of last year had the highest HIV infection rate in the industrialized world. Of 257 Vancouver addicts who initially tested negative for HIV, 24 had been exposed to the virus within six months, despite the fact that 23 of them reported regularly obtaining sterile equipment from the NEP. Sharing of contaminated needles remains a "normative" behavior among addicts, this study's authors concluded. Wide distribution of clean needles does not change this "alarming" fact.

David Tell, *Weekly Standard*, May 4, 1998.

Another significant report was published in 1993 by the University of California and funded by the U.S. Centers for Disease Control. A panel reviewed 21 studies on the impact of NEPs on HIV infection rates. But the best the authors could say for the programs was that none showed a higher prevalence of HIV among program clients.

Even those results don't mean much. Panel members rated the scientific quality of the studies on a five-point scale: one meant "not valid," three "acceptable," and five "excellent." Only two of the studies earned ratings of three or higher. Of those, neither showed a reduction in HIV levels. No wonder the authors concluded that the data simply do not, and for methodological reasons probably cannot, provide clear evidence that needle exchanges decrease HIV infection rates.

Numerous Methodological Problems

The most extensive review of needle-exchange studies was commissioned in 1993 by the U.S. Department of Health and Human Services (HHS), which directed the National Academy of Sciences (NAS) to oversee the project. Their report, "Preventing HIV Transmission: The Role of Sterile Needles and Bleach," was issued in 1995 and set off a political firestorm.

"Well-implemented needle-exchange programs can be effective in preventing the spread of HIV and do not increase the use of illegal drugs," a 15-member panel concluded. It recommended lifting the ban on federal funding for NEPs, along with laws against possession of injection paraphernalia. The NAS report has emerged as the bible for true believers of needle exchange.

It is not likely to stand the test of time. A truly scientific trial testing the ability of NEPs to reduce needle-sharing and HIV transmission would set up two similar, randomly selected populations of drug users. One group would be given access to free needles, the other would not. Researchers would follow them for at least a year, taking periodic blood tests.

None of the studies reviewed by NAS researchers, however, were designed in this way. Their methodological problems are legion: Sample sizes are often too small to be statistically meaningful. Participants are self-selected, so that the more health-conscious could be skewing the results. As many as 60 percent of study participants drop out. And researchers rely on self-reporting, a notoriously untrustworthy tool.

"Nobody has done the basic science yet," says David Murray, the research director of the Statistical Assessment Service, a watchdog group in Washington, D.C. "If this were the FDA applying the standard for a new drug, they would block it right there."

The NAS panel admitted its conclusions were not based on reviews of well-designed trials. Such studies, the authors agreed, simply do not exist. Not to worry, they said: "The limitations of individual studies do not necessarily preclude us from being able to reach scientifically valid conclusions." When all of the studies are considered together, they argued, the results are compelling.

"That's like tossing a bunch of broken Christmas ornaments in a box and claiming you have something nice and new and usable," Murray says. "What you have is a lot of broken ornaments." Two of the three physicians on the NAS panel, Lawrence Brown and Herbert Kleber, agree. They deny their report established anything like a scientific link between lower HIV rates and needle exchanges. "The existing data is flawed," says Kleber, executive vice president for medical research at Columbia University. "NEPs may, in theory, be effective, but the data doesn't prove that they are."

> *"The [Medical University of South Carolina] demonstrated well-documented special needs in treating and preventing cocaine use by pregnant women."*

Drug Tests of Pregnant Women Are Necessary

Robert H. Hood

In the following viewpoint, Robert H. Hood contends that the Medical University of South Carolina (MUSC) was justified in its decision to test pregnant women for cocaine use. Hood, writing on behalf of Charleston, South Carolina, in a Supreme Court case, argues that these tests are valid because of the serious health risks to both mother and developing fetus caused by maternal drug use. In addition, he claims that the drug testing policy helps women overcome substance abuse problems and is not arbitrary or discriminatory. Hood is the founder and senior partner at the Hood Law Firm in South Carolina.

As you read, consider the following questions:

1. As stated by the author, what is the first step in the special needs analysis?
2. What was the goal of the MUSC Medical Center, in Hood's opinion?
3. According to statistics cited by Hood, how many of the women affected by the medical center's policy did not test positive for drugs a second time?

Robert H. Hood, "Drug-Testing of Pregnant Women," *Supreme Court Debates*, vol. 3, November 2000, pp. 237–49.

[The Supreme] Court has recognized that in certain cases, the government may have "special needs," beyond normal law enforcement goals, which make the usual warrant and probable cause requirement impracticable.

The special needs doctrine applies where there is an important or compelling special need founded on a concrete danger. Ultimately, the reasonableness of the search must be evaluated by balancing the public interest and the effectiveness of the search in advancing that interest against the individual privacy expectations and the degree of intrusion suffered by the individuals.

In upholding the MUSC [Medical University of South Carolina] policy, the court of appeals correctly applied the principles and adhered to the parameters set by this Court. The evidence demonstrates that the drug screens were medically necessary for the treatment of the maternity patients and their children and that the epidemic of cocaine use by pregnant women and the attendant public health problems created important special needs beyond normal law enforcement goals.

The evidence also establishes that the MUSC urine testing policy was effective in addressing these special needs and that the intrusion on the Petitioners' privacy expectations was minimal. Therefore, the court of appeals properly found that the searches were reasonable and judgment should be affirmed on that ground alone. . . .

A Clinically Based Need

The first step in the special needs analysis is the determination of whether the search serves a special governmental need beyond normal law enforcement needs. Contrary to the Petitioners' assertions, the policy was not merely a symbolic opposition to drug use as in *Chandler v. Miller*. Rather, the MUSC Medical Center demonstrated well-documented special needs in treating and preventing cocaine use by pregnant women.

The incontrovertible evidence is that both the obstetrical and neonatal medical staff had a clinically based need for the information in order to manage the pregnancy and treat the newborns. The evidence also demonstrated that medical communities in the City of Charleston, other areas of the State of South Carolina, and across this Nation were experiencing serious maternal and neonatal health problems as a result of the epidemic of prenatal drug abuse.

The Petitioners attempt to deny the existence of the problem and/or minimize its impact. However, the Petitioners' own expert, Dr. Ira Chasnoff, testified before Congress in 1989 that there had been a rapid rise in reported instances of cocaine use during pregnancy and something needed to be done immediately about the problem.

Since the "special need" was uniquely medical in nature, it was appropriately addressed on the frontline by medical personnel that could best identify the at-risk patients and most effectively implement a policy to prevent or treat prenatal drug abuse.

The words of Justice Powell in his concurrence in *New Jersey v. T.L.O.* illustrate how special relationships—such as those between health care providers and their patients—can establish a basis for recognizing special needs exceptions to the warrant/probable cause requirement:

> Law enforcement officers function as adversaries of criminal suspects. These officers have the responsibility to investigate criminal activity, to locate and arrest those who violate our laws, and to facilitate the charging and bringing of such persons to trial. Rarely does this type of adversarial relationship exist between school authorities and pupils. Instead, there is a commonality of interests between teachers and their pupils. The attitude of the typical teacher is one of personal responsibility for the student's welfare as well as for his education.

The Court in *Griffin v. Wisconsin* (1987) also found it pertinent that the primary role of a probation officer was not to investigate criminal activity, but to supervise his client with the goal of assuring that the probation served as a period of genuine rehabilitation.

Common Interests

By the same token, health care providers and patients do not stand in an adversarial relationship to each other. Instead, there is a commonality of interests between medical personnel and their patients. In maternity cases, the medical personnel and the patients share common interests in the health of both the mother and her child.

The medical staff did not conduct the drug screens for the purpose of investigating criminal activity. The purpose was to provide proper medical treatment to their patients. During pregnancy, so many factors affect the health of the mother, the course of the labor and delivery, and the health of the child that the medical staff cannot adequately treat the pregnant patient or manage the pregnancy without such critical information as the patient's use of illegal drugs.

Obstetrical Complications Associated with Substance Abuse

Foetal wastage resulting in
  Spontaneous abortion
  Intrauterine death
  Amnionitis
  Chorioamnionitis
  Gestational diabetes
  Premature rupture of membranes and septicaemia

Placental disorders
  Abruption
  Infarction
  Insufficiency

Foetal growth retardation

Premature labour with or without breech presentation

L.P. Finnegan, *Bulletin on Narcotics*, vol. XLVI, no. 1, 1994.

The opinion of the court of appeals cannot fairly be read, as the Petitioners assert, to establish any dangerous precedent that would permit law enforcement to engage in warrantless searches for just any and every health or safety reason. The court of appeals adhered to this Court's decisions in *Vernonia School District 475 v. Acton* and *Chandler* in stressing that the governmental need must be "compelling" and that "the hazard giving rise to the alleged special need must be a concrete danger, not merely a hypothetical one." The court of appeals correctly found that: "In light of the documented health hazards of maternal cocaine use and the resulting drain on public resources, MUSC officials unquestionably possessed a substantial interest in taking steps to reduce cocaine use by pregnant women."

The court of appeals decision is not a radical departure from the parameters set by the Court. To the contrary, it squarely fits within those parameters as a clear case of special needs sufficient to sustain the MUSC policy.

In comparing the range of documentation and substantiation of the special needs, this case clearly aligns most closely with *Vernonia*, where the school district presented solid evidence to document the existence and extent of the problem of drug abuse by its students and the harmful consequences to school discipline and the students' health. Unlike in *Chandler*, the special need to protect pregnant women and their children from prenatal cocaine abuse is not merely symbolic, but fully demonstrated by the evidence of an epidemic causing serious public health problems.

Beyond Law Enforcement

The Petitioners complain about the collaboration with law enforcement and argue that any special needs search must be totally divorced from any law enforcement activity. However, this argument directly conflicts with the Court's repeated references to "'special needs' beyond normal law enforcement."—*Griffin*.

Notwithstanding the references to the restricted use of the drug test results in *National Treasury Employees Union v. Von Raab, Skinner v. Railway Labor Executives Association*, and *Acton*, the Court has never said that the results of a special needs search cannot be turned over to law enforcement. Notably, in *T.L.O.*, which came before the Court on appeal of the juvenile criminal case, the Court found no reason to invalidate the search because the fruits were ultimately turned over to the police.

Here, the MUSC Medical Center had a primary, clinical need to identify cocaine use that was wholly beyond normal law enforcement goals. However, under State law, prenatal illegal drug use constitutes child abuse. Thus, once in possession of evidence of cocaine use, State law mandated that the MUSC medical staff report such cases to law enforcement or the Department of Social Services. Nothing in the prior decisions of this Court intimates that disclosure of such information under mandatory reporting statutes would invalidate an otherwise legitimate special needs search. Further, this case does not present any evidence, direct or inferential, that the MUSC Medical Center's goal of protecting the health of its maternity patients and their children was merely a pretext to prosecute cocaine addicts. The record establishes that there was a very real medical epidemic and the Medical Center's only goal was to manage the pregnancies of its maternity patients and prevent maternal and infant injuries arising from prenatal cocaine abuse.

The Medical Center had already attempted a protocol that proved ineffective and it was the substance abuse counselors that proposed the coercive element necessary to make the policy work. The purpose of the urine drug tests was not to prosecute the drug laws; rather, the threat of prosecution was but a tool in implementing a policy that would prove to be effective in discouraging their patients from prenatal cocaine abuse.

A Successful Policy

The second step is an assessment of the effectiveness of the policy in meeting the identified, important special needs. As the court of appeals found, the urine drug screens were effective in identifying cocaine use which met the clinical needs. In addition, a decline in the number of positive drug screens, and fewer associated medical complications, demonstrated that the policy effectively met the broader need to discourage prenatal cocaine use.

Evidence established that the policy had a 90 percent success rate: 223 of the 253 pregnant women who tested positive the first time completed substance abuse treatment and did not test positive a second time. Of the 30 who did test positive a second time and were arrested, 28 successfully completed substance abuse treatment through the pretrial intervention program. Most telling is the testimony of many of these Petitioners that they had finally beaten their cocaine habits.

Despite this evidence, the Petitioners claim that the policy was ineffective in promoting fetal health because of what they allege as its "faulty design" in focusing only on cocaine use and by employing a punitive approach to treatment.

The Petitioners assert that the policy was "medically senseless" because it did not address other drugs that also pose risks of harm to the infant. Such assertion is disingenuous in light of the fact that their own expert testified that at the time, cocaine use had been identified as a particularly critical problem—both in terms of its epidemic scope and devastating consequences. Similarly, their contention that the punitive approach drives women away from prenatal care and treatment disregards the record evidence to the contrary.

Further, the Respondents' decision to focus on cocaine use was a rational discretionary policy decision not subject to second-guessing. This Court has recognized that policymakers are not constitutionally obligated to tackle complex problems with full-scope, comprehensive programs. Rather, they may take a step-by-step approach and address that phase of the problem which they adjudge most acute at the time.

Likewise, the decision to employ a punitive, "carrot and stick" approach to discouraging cocaine use was rationally based on consultation with substance abuse counselors. And, although the evidence rebuts the claim that this discouraged some pregnant women from seeking treatment, any such indirect impact does not invalidate the policy.

The Policy Is Not Discriminatory

There is rarely, if ever, a single perfect solution to a complex problem such as prenatal drug abuse. This Court has "frequently recognized that individual States have broad latitude in experimenting with possible solutions to problems of vital local concern."—*Whalen v. Roe* (1977). This Court has also stated that "the law need not be in every respect logically consistent with its aims to be constitutional. It is enough that there is an evil at hand for correction, and that it might be thought that the particular legislative measure was a rational way to correct it."—*Williamson v. Lee Optical of Oklahoma* (1955).

It is for the policymakers to balance the benefits and risks of proposed solutions, and their decisions are reviewable by the courts only for arbitrariness and capriciousness or invidious discrimination. Experts in a given field may disagree over techniques to be employed to deal with a serious danger, but "for purposes of the Fourth Amendment analysis, the choice among such reasonable alternatives remains with the governmental officials"—not the courts.—*Michigan State Department of Police v. Sitz* (1990).

The policy was the product of an orderly and studied attempt to deal with a specific problem of epidemic proportions. There was nothing unreasonable or discriminatory in their identification of cocaine as a particularly critical problem or their decision to focus on that illegal drug to the exclusion of other illegal (or legal) substances which pose risks to maternal and fetal health.

*"[The] data clearly show racial and
socioeconomic bias in South Carolina . . .
in the application of criminal sanctions for
perinatal substance abuse."*

Drug Tests of Pregnant Women Are Discriminatory

Mary Faith Marshall

The Medical University of South Carolina's policy of screening pregnant women for drug use as part of prenatal care is racist, Mary Faith Marshall asserts in the following viewpoint. According to Marshall, the policy targets substance use by lower-class minorities, who are more likely to use cocaine, while ignoring alcohol and drug abuse among wealthier white females. She claims that black women are more likely to be reported for drug use than their white counterparts and that such discrimination is indicative of other coercive obstetrical policies. Marshall is a professor of medicine and bioethics at Kansas University Medical Center in Lawrence.

As you read, consider the following questions:
1. What did the South Carolina Supreme Court rule in *State of S.C. v. Whitner?*
2. According to Marshall, why are poor women at a greater risk for drug detection?
3. What percentage of women smokes cigarettes during pregnancy, as stated by the author?

Mary Faith Marshall, prepared statement to the House Subcommittee on National Security, International Affairs, and Criminal Justice, July 23, 1998, pp. 129–35.

The State of South Carolina has been more active than any other state in criminalizing substance abuse by pregnant women. In Charleston, the Medical University of South Carolina developed an extensive collaboration with local police and the prosecutor's office. Under the Medical University policy, information regarding pregnant women who tested positive for illegal drugs in the hospital's obstetrics clinic was turned over to the police and the prosecutor. The policy did not apply to private patients or to patients at any other health care facility in the Charleston area. For women who tested positive, freedom from arrest and prosecution was conditioned on compliance with mandatory prenatal and substance abuse treatment. Forty-one women were arrested under the policy, (all but one of whom were Black). Ten of the women brought charges against the Medical University, the police department, and the prosecutor. Notwithstanding unanimous opposition to such collaborations by professional organizations, many of which filed amicus briefs for the plaintiffs, citing long standing clinical norms such as privacy and confidentiality, informed consent, and the right to refuse treatment, a federal jury dismissed all charges against the hospital, the police, and the prosecutor.

On July 15, 1996 (in *State of S.C. v. Whitner*) the South Carolina Supreme Court established that a viable fetus can be considered a person under the child abuse and neglect statute. Thus, a pregnant woman may be held criminally liable for any action during her pregnancy that would "endanger the life, health or comfort" of her fetus. The High Court explicitly noted that the statute applies to acts that are either legal or illegal. In June, 1998, the United States Supreme Court refused, without comment, to hear the Whitner appeal. Since that date, two S.C. women whose newborns tested positive for marijuana and cocaine respectively have been charged with unlawful conduct to a child.

Racial and Socioeconomic Discrimination

A prevalence study conducted by the South Carolina governor's office found a high incidence of barbiturate, marijuana and opiate use among pregnant white women. Data from the Medical University of South Carolina's data bank on newborn prenatal screening showed an equal distribution of drug use among white and Black patients. A study by Tribble et al at the Medical University of South Carolina showed that "while equivalent proportions of black and white populations were drug positive (2.52% blacks, 2.54% whites), black mothers were more likely to use cocaine than white mothers (1.25% blacks, 0.28% whites)." Their data also suggested that the cocaine screening policy was associated with a decrease in the utilization of prenatal care by women who screened drug positive. Nevertheless, the vast majority of prosecutions in South Carolina and other states have been against Black women. Of the 41 women arrested under the Medical University of South Carolina's Interagency Policy, 40 were black, and the sole white woman had a black boyfriend (as was noted in her medical record). Of 109 women charged with criminal child abuse for perinatal substance abuse by the Greenville, S.C. solicitor, 101 were crack cocaine addicts, and 86 of them were Black.

These data clearly show racial and socioeconomic bias in South Carolina and throughout the United States in the application of criminal sanctions for perinatal substance abuse. These data mirror national statistics on the overall disproportionate impact of the criminal justice system on the poor and on racial minorities. There are currently more than one million inmates incarcerated in prisons in the United States. Since 1980 the number of inmates in the U.S. has doubled, and the number of female inmates has tripled (the rate of growth for female inmates has exceeded that for males each year since 1981). Most of these arrests have been for nonviolent, drug-related offenses. Most of those arrested, convicted and imprisoned are poor minorities.

A recent Department of Justice survey investigating the characteristics of women inmates reveals that:

> Women in United States jails are usually in their late twenties, close to half of them have never married, and about half have completed high school. Most are unemployed, use illegal drugs, are black or are Spanish-speaking, have children under eighteen, and have previously been convicted at least once.

Separation from their children is a common occurrence among women inmates. Approximately two-thirds of female

118

(adult and adolescent) inmates have children under eighteen. These females are most often single parents whose children were living with them prior to their incarceration

Drug Screening and Reporting

Not surprisingly, this profile mirrors that of women arrested for perinatal substance abuse. Since 1985, more than 240 women in 35 states have been criminally prosecuted for using illegal drugs or alcohol during pregnancy. Between 70% and 80% of these women are minorities. Many factors influence this discriminatory approach. Poor women (a category that is inherently disproportionately Black) are at greater risk for drug detection because of their necessarily close relationship with social service and other government agencies. Greater scrutiny by government officials results in disproportionately higher rates of drug screening and reporting. Lack of prenatal care, frequently a trigger for pre- or postnatal drug screening, correlates directly with race and income, as Black women are twice as likely to receive late or no prenatal care than white women because of poverty and other logistical barriers.

A landmark study in Pinellas County, Florida, in which women presenting for obstetrical care at public health clinics

Unfair and Coercive Policies

Policies that coerce or punish pregnant women purport to protect the public's health. On closer reflection, however, they may be harmful and reflect subtle forms of discrimination. Conscripting health care professionals to perform law enforcement undermines patient trust, which may lead to a reduction in prenatal care and even in the overall use of health services. Further, policies or laws that coerce or punish pregnant women may encourage more abortions; a woman who must choose between abortion and incarceration may prefer the former.

These policies raise questions of fairness because they are applied exclusively to women and predominantly to poor women of color. Men who endanger the health of the fetus through spousal abuse, for example, are not subjected to special penalties related to fetal protection.

Lawrence O. Gostin, *Hastings Center Report*, September/October 2001.

and private physicians' offices were anonymously tested for drug use, found that **Black women were ten times more likely to be reported for positive drug screens while pregnant than white women.** This finding is especially disturbing given the results from the same study that drug use prevalence was similar across racial and socioeconomic groups (drug use among white women was actually slightly higher [15.4%] than for Black women [14.1%]—a finding consistent with the national trend in illegal drug use). Studies in other states have revealed similar evidence of racial bias in perinatal drug screening and reporting despite similar prevalence rates of substance abuse across racial lines. Consistent with these data, a recent General Accounting Office (GAO) report found that infants of non-Medicaid patients in private hospitals were screened less often than infants in public hospitals.

Racial and socioeconomic discrimination in the obstetrical realm go beyond perinatal substance abuse. Historically, most coercive approaches to obstetrical care have involved poor minorities. Such coercion includes the vast majority of court-ordered obstetrical interventions, including forced cesarean section. A survey published in the *New England Journal of Medicine* in 1987 showed that of the eighteen cases in which court orders allowed coercive obstetrical interventions (out of twenty-one cases petitioned), eighty-one percent of the pregnant patients were minorities. Socioeconomic status played an even greater role, as each of the women was either receiving public assistance or was being treated at a public hospital.

Illegal and Legal Drugs

Further evidence of racial and socioeconomic bias in the application of criminal statutes to perinatal behavior is seen in arbitrary selection of certain types of drugs for reporting or criminal prosecution. Criminal sanctions are imposed against women who use illegal drugs much more frequently than those who use legal drugs. Certain illegal drugs, such as crack cocaine, heroin, and marijuana, are often specifically targeted for screening programs while illegal drugs such as powdered cocaine, crank (methamphetamine) or non-physician-ordered psychotherapeutics are largely ignored. Pregnant women who use targeted drugs, such as crack cocaine, are much more likely to be reported and arrested than pregnant women who use non-targeted drugs, such as powdered cocaine, narcotic analgesics, and psychotherapeutic agents.

Prevalence studies demonstrate clear racial and socioeconomic dividing lines among use of various substances. Data from the 1992 NIDA report *National Pregnancy & Health Survey: Drug Use Among Women Delivering Livebirths* provide national estimates of the prevalence and patterns of use of illicit drugs, cigarettes, and alcohol before, during, and after pregnancy. These findings estimate that 5.5 percent of women use an illegal drug sometime during their pregnancies. The most frequently used illegal drug is marijuana (2.9 percent of pregnant women). Psychotherapeutic drugs without physician orders comprise the second largest category of illegal drug use (1.5 percent), while cocaine is used by 1.1 percent of pregnant women. Use of drugs such as hashish, methamphetamine, heroin, methadone, inhalants and hallucinogens is much less frequent.

Much higher percentages of pregnant women use legal drugs during pregnancy than illegal drugs. Cigarettes are the most frequently used substances (20.4 percent), with alcohol following closely behind (18.8 percent). Usage patterns of these drugs tend to be distributed along socioeconomic lines, with a higher incidence of alcohol use in the highest income group, and a higher incidence of cigarette use in the lower income group. Alcohol is the only commonly abused substance certain to cause congenital anomalies in some infants, and Fetal Alcohol Syndrome is the leading cause of mental retardation in the United States. Sociodemographic variables also account for significant differences in usage rates between legal and illegal drugs. Marijuana, cocaine and cigarettes are used more frequently by women who are unmarried, unemployed, have less than sixteen years of education, and rely on public assistance for health care. Alcohol, on the other hand, is primarily used by women who are employed, have sixteen years or more of education, and have private health insurance. Methamphetamine is used primarily by white women (as opposed to black women, or men in general), and some hospitals—especially those in the west and midwest—are seeing larger percentages of newborns testing positive for methamphetamine than for crack cocaine. Cocaine use divides along racial lines, with powdered cocaine preferred by white women, and crack cocaine preferred by Black women. This reflects the earlier income-related demographic, as crack cocaine use is generally associated with poverty, homelessness, and inner-city Black communities.

Clearly, pregnant women who use marijuana and nonordered prescription drugs comprise the largest category of illicit perinatal substance abusers. Women who fall into this demographic, however, are not the ones most affected by criminal interventions.

*"I tried to keep an open mind [about AA]
no matter what anyone said and how
stupid I thought it was. That probably
saved my life."*

Alcoholics Anonymous Can Reduce the Problems Caused by Drinking

Anonymous

One of the most well known substance abuse treatment programs is the one developed by Alcoholics Anonymous. In the following viewpoint, a member of Alcoholics Anonymous contends that the organization, whose program does not permit even limited consumption of alcohol, helped save her life. According to the author, treatments such as controlled-drinking programs, psychiatry, and biofeedback failed to reduce her compulsion to drink. She asserts that although she was initially reluctant to become a member of Alcoholics Anonymous, she is glad she kept an open mind because the meetings and literature have helped her control her drinking problem. The anonymous author of this viewpoint is a lawyer.

As you read, consider the following questions:

1. According to the author, how did her friends describe her behavior when she drank?
2. How did the author sum up her attitude toward Alcoholics Anonymous, following her initial return to the organization?
3. According to the author, how was her final hangover different from all the ones that had preceded it?

Anonymous, *Alcoholics Anonymous: The Story of How Many Thousands of Men and Women Have Recovered from Alcoholism*. New York: Alcoholics Anonymous World Services, Inc., 2001. Copyright © 2001 by Alcoholics Anonymous World Services, Inc. Reproduced by permission.

When I was a newly minted lawyer starting out in the practice of criminal law, there were five of us in our law office. My favorite lawyer was the eccentric, disheveled, wild-eyed Irish law professor who was brilliant or crazy, depending on your point of view, constantly cleaning out his pipe bowl with a black fingernail and tossing back vodka martinis whenever he got the chance. Then there was the new but world-weary litigation lawyer who told endless tales of his former life of white wine and bouillabaisse under the Mediterranean sun as he conducted his exporting business on the Riviera. Why would he leave such an ideal, wine-drenched job in sunny climes to slog away at law school? I kept wondering. There was also a giant good-hearted bear of a man, who today is a judge, who spent more time listening and helping others than he did practicing criminal law. Into this office landed a pair of know-it-all, fast-acting, but not too experienced young lawyers: my husband and me.

Within a dozen years, three of these five promising lawyers were dead from alcoholism, struck down at the peak of their careers. The judge is still and always has been a sober judge. And I somehow unwittingly, and even while drinking, turned into a corporate counsel and later, thankfully, became a member of Alcoholics Anonymous. The professor's kidneys gave out from one too many martinis; the exporting lawyer kept drinking until he died, despite a liver transplant; my ex-husband died in a fire on what was to be, he had said, his last drunk before going to A.A. *again*, when I was ten years sober. I have been to too many premature funerals due to our good friend alcohol.

A Lifetime of Drinking

My husband and I met and married in law school in a romantic haze of alcohol, twinkling lights, and much promise. We stood out as the only young married couple in our class. We worked and played hard, camped and hiked and skied, threw fabulous parties for our sophisticated friends, and prided ourselves on staying away from drugs. In fact, it was fear that kept me away from drugs—fear that I might not get called to the bar (that's the other bar, the legal one) if I were convicted of possession of illegal street drugs. More importantly, my best friend was wonderful, powerful alcohol, and I loved it.

Until I was four years old, I lived upstairs from a tavern, where I saw a few drunks bounced around. My mother worked for relatives who also lived over the tavern, and whoever had time looked after me. Despite my pleas, my mother married a violent man, and we moved away to a life that made my tavern life look really holy. I kept running away back to the tavern until it was demolished. I still fondly look at pictures of that place.

By the age of fourteen I had my first drunk, which ended in a minor police visit to my home. By the age of eighteen I was a daily drinker, and by age twenty-one I had my first year-long binge in France, which I euphemistically referred to as my study year abroad. I came home very sick and drunk. A few months later I went to bed with a bottle of Scotch one night and decided I would go to law school. If you are having trouble, try something that is even more difficult, to "show them." That was my philosophy. It was enough to drive me to drink, and it did.

At law school we used to drink a lot of beer in student pubs, debating whether rocks had souls and what was the nature of the judicial process, as though it had never been considered before. As new lawyers, my husband and I eagerly beavered in the office early in the morning before running off to court to fearlessly defend the downtrodden. Lunch was the training ground for the perpetual quest for the best martini—usually two or three of them, good for taking away the knot that by this time had permanently lodged itself in my stomach. (I didn't know that it represented fear and that I was not a fearless defender after all.) Afternoons would be full of creative legal arguments in court. If court finished early, maybe we'd make it back to the office, maybe not.

Evenings we drank with the best of them: lawyers, writers, media types, everyone vying to tell the best stories, which of course got funnier and funnier the more we drank and the later it got. When I drank, the fear evaporated and I became articulate and apparently very, very funny—or so they said then. Years later I drank so much that I was no longer funny. But at the time, the drinks and the stories and the camaraderie were as wonderful as I was witty. We would get home to sleep by one or two in the morning, and the next day we would be up early to start all over again. The fortitude and resilience of youth made us invincible.

Seeking a Solution

Unfortunately, by the time we thought it was time to have a "real life" and maybe start a family, the marriage disintegrated. I was then twenty-eight years old, getting divorced, drinking all the time, and seeing a psychiatrist three times a week, trying to solve my problem, whatever it was.

I thought I had found part of the answer when I stumbled into a private controlled-drinking program, which helped me, during the initial thirty-day mandatory period of abstinence, to hook a very large rug, row by row, well into many late nights. "One more row!" I kept saying, gritting my teeth against a drink. My period of abstinence also helped me get a better job in the corporate world, away from all those hard-drinking criminal lawyers, and a new three-story, four-bedroom house. Just what every single woman needs! It helped me to quit the psychiatrist. During this abstinence, I also got out of a sick relationship, which reproduced the violence of my childhood.

Incredibly, I did not connect the improved manageability of my life in this short period of abstinence to the absence of booze. It didn't matter in the long run, because unfortunately, I started to get drunk again. I recall being fixated on that first glass of wine I was allowed to drink the day my coach informed me that I was ready to start drinking in controlled fashion. My tongue was almost hanging out.

Many drunks later, I tried everything else I could find: more therapy, different psychiatrists (it was always to be the next one who would solve my problem), biofeedback, relaxation exercises, Antabuse, lots of self-help books from Freud to Jung, to every current fad that was published or taught. All to no avail, of course, because I'd always end up drunk.

Came the day when I realized that I couldn't keep dragging myself off to work in the morning and spending half the energy of every day concealing the fact that I was a barely functioning drunk. I would go home to drink until I passed out, come to in the middle of the night terrified, listen to the radio, and get worldwide telephonitis, finally dozing off at dawn, just in time to be awakened by the alarm and start the process all over again. I gave up on relationships of any significance, saw my friends less, and stopped committing myself to most social occasions because I could never count on being sober. More and more, I just worked and went home to drink—and the drinking was starting to outstrip the working.

Alcoholics Anonymous

One day I was so hungover at lunchtime I called a friend and had a little cry. "I've tried everything and nothing works," I said, reciting my litany of doctors and different therapies. I did not remember that thirteen years earlier, when I was twenty-one years old, I had attended a few meetings of Alcoholics Anonymous after waking up one morning not knowing where I was. I had just started law school and was terrified most of the time, so I went on a binge to quell the fear, which only got worse. I have no idea what made me go to A.A. way back then. But there were no young people at the meetings, and people kept marveling at how young and fresh I looked. (No one at A.A. said that when I came back thirteen years later.)

My friend suggested that we contact a man she knew who was a member of Alcoholics Anonymous, and I agreed to call him. "Perhaps he could call you," she said helpfully, which was the key, because by that night I was just fine and didn't need any outside help aside from a drink or two. But he kept phoning and bothering me about going to a meeting. When he told me he went to A.A. meetings three or four times a week, I thought, poor man, he has nothing better to do. What a boring life it must be for him, running around to A.A. meetings with nothing to drink! Boring indeed: no bouncing off walls, no falling down stairs, no regular trips to hospital emergency rooms, no lost cars, and on and on.

My first meeting back at A.A. was on an unseasonably hot June night, but there was not a cool drink in sight in that church basement. The smoke could have choked a horse (today, it is much improved), and a fanatical woman with smiling bright eyes eagerly explained to me that they had this

Controlled Drinking and Diminished Capacity

There is no good evidence supporting the effectiveness of controlled drinking for chronic alcoholics. Why should it be offered as an alternative to abstinence training? However, it is logically possible that a small number of people suffering from alcohol abuse or alcohol dependence (alcoholism) could choose moderation over abstinence and benefit.

But, self-selection of treatment is currently impossible for many important reasons:. . .

[One] problem is the patient's diminished capacity; his or her inability to fully understand the information presented, integrate it and determine its relevance to self. Diminished capacity is common in alcohol-abusing patients due to the neurochemical effects of alcohol, either in terms of brain damage and consequent neuropsychological deficits, depression, panic, polydrug use and more.

A patient with diminished capacity is not fully autonomous, and is incapable of providing a valid informed consent and a reasoned treatment self-selection.

Irving Maltzman, *Counselor*, December 2000.

important book I should buy. Thinking that they were doing the book promotion because they needed the money, I said firmly, "I'll give you the money, but I don't want your book!" Which about sums up my attitude and explains why, for the next few months, I continued to get drunk in spite of dragging my body to meetings every few days. I would stare at the large vodka bottle in my kitchen cupboard and say, "You won't get me!" but it did; I always lost the battle and ended up drunk.

The Final Hangover

My last hangover was on a Friday before a long summer weekend. I had struggled through the day feeling small and hopeless, hiding the trembling of my hands when I had to sign documents, and desperately working to wrap my tongue around words during meetings. Later that Friday night, after an agonizingly long workday, I was dragging myself up the deserted street thinking that the whole world, except for me, had someplace to go on that long weekend, and what's more, they all had someone to go with.

The first difference between that night and all the others

was that I did not immediately go directly to a bar to get lubricated or home with my regular giant weekend supply of booze. Instead I went to my club to swim, where strangely enough I also did not drink. I was so hungover that I had to give up trying to swim and instead wrapped myself in a bathrobe and sat in a dark corner of the locker room lounge for two hours, feeling desperately sorry for myself.

I don't know what happened during those two hours, but close to eight o'clock, I leaped up, jumped into my clothes, and raced off to a meeting I'd had no intention of attending. It was a bit like getting a rap on the head with an invisible hammer and having my brain flip over, because the meeting seemed to be radically different from the last time I had been there. The people looked animatedly alive, the weirdos who had been attending before were absent that night, and the books on display actually looked interesting. I bought the book *Alcoholics Anonymous*, listened intently, and then, for the first time, I went for coffee with those people and listened some more.

Late that night at home, there was a presence in the room with me, even though I lived alone. The next morning I knew I didn't have to drink. That night I went to a Step meeting where they discussed Step Two, "Came to believe that a Power greater than ourselves could restore us to sanity," and I actually talked about God, the one who had abandoned me when I was very little, very frightened, and very hurt. In the weeks and months that followed, I did everything that was suggested to me. I went to a meeting every day, read the books and literature, and got a sponsor who told me to have a quiet time every morning and try to pray and meditate or at least sit still for a few minutes, before racing off for the day. Since I prided myself on adhering to the intellectual principle of not having contempt for anything prior to investigation, I tried to keep an open mind no matter what anyone said and how stupid I thought it was. That probably saved my life. . . .

Staying Protected

Many years later, although alcohol is not part of my life and I no longer have the compulsion to drink, it can still occur to me what a good drink tastes like and what it can do for me, from my stand-at-attention alcoholic taste buds right down to my stretched out tingling toes. As my A.A. sponsor used to point out, such thoughts are like red flags, telling me that something is not right, that I am stretched beyond my sober limit. It's time to get back to basic A.A. and see what needs changing. That special relationship with alcohol will always be there, waiting to seduce me again. I can stay protected by continuing to be an active member of A.A.

"It is possible to distinguish between safe and hazardous behavior, between responsible and reckless drinking."

Harm-Reduction Approaches Can Reduce the Problems Caused by Drinking

Marcus Grant and Eric Single

In the following viewpoint, Marcus Grant and Eric Single assert that harm-reduction policies can help reduce the problems associated with alcohol consumption. According to Grant and Single, these policies recognize that drinking is not always harmful, while acknowledging that steps need to be taken to reduce adverse consequences such as drunk driving, consumption of potentially deadly nonbeverage alcohol, and violence. In addition, they argue that the harm-reduction approach does not restrict the freedom of the majority in order to protect the irresponsible or vulnerable behavior of a smaller population. Grant is the president of the International Center for Alcohol Politics, an organization that encourages dialogue in the beverage alcohol industry; Singer is a senior policy associate at the Canadian Centre on Substance Abuse, a national agency that promotes debate on drug and alcohol abuse issues.

As you read, consider the following questions:
1. As stated by the authors, what prompted the development of harm-reduction policies?
2. According to Grant and Single, what is the purpose of server intervention programs?

Marcus Grant and Eric Single, "Shifting the Paradigm: Reducing Harm and Promoting Beneficial Patterns," *Drinking Patterns and Their Consequences*, edited by Marcus Grant and Jorge Litvak, Washington, DC: Taylor & Francis, 1998. Copyright © 1998 by International Center for Alcohol Policies. Reproduced by permission.

Growing attention has been devoted to harm-reduction measures in a number of public health areas. Harm reduction was developed as an approach to deal with problems associated with illicit drug use, particularly the spread of HIV infection among intravenous drug users. In this context, and in contrast to abstinence-oriented approaches, harm reduction focuses on reducing the consequences of drug use rather than eliminating drug use. It seeks to adopt practical rather than idealized goals. Thus, focus is placed on safer use patterns rather than the deterrence of use per se. Needle exchange programs and other harm-reduction measures have often faced resistance from those who are understandably concerned that such practices may condone or facilitate drug use and thus increase drug problems. But evaluation studies have shown that harm-reduction programs have generally succeeded in reducing the spread of AIDS and other diseases and in helping many dependent users to lead normal lives as productive members of society, without leading to increases in levels of drug use. Thus harm reduction has been a very successful movement, both politically and epidemiologically, in the area of HIV prevention.

Applying the Harm-Reduction Concept

Harm-reduction measures have expanded to a broad variety of programming aimed not only at reducing the spread of AIDS and other communicable diseases but also at other adverse consequences of drug use. In the case of illicit drug use, there remains for some the ethical issue of whether harm-reduction approaches condone, or could be perceived to condone, a behavior that is against the law. However, this is clearly not a relevant consideration with respect to alcohol consumption except under some legally defined minimum drinking age or in relation to other behaviors such as driving a motor vehicle.

This is an important distinction. It enables the harm-reduction approach to alcohol problems to be coupled logically with efforts to promote those drinking patterns that maximize benefits, whether expressed in terms of individual health and quality of life or in terms of enhanced socioeconomic functioning. For most drinkers, the vast majority of the time, harm remains distant and improbable. However, . . . the concept is relevant to all. Thus, as it applies to alcohol, harm reduction refers to policies and programs that focus on reducing the adverse consequences of drinking rather than measures aimed at restricting access to alcohol. As such, it shifts the focus toward those drinking patterns associated with adverse consequences, rather than assuming that all drinking is equally likely to lead to harm. Indeed, it is not assumed that level of drinking is necessarily the most useful distinguishing characteristic.

If less is always better (as the single-distribution approach assumes) then abstinence would logically be best of all. Harm-reduction measures, by contrast, presume that drinking will take place. This does not imply approval or disapproval of drinking; that drinking occurs is simply accepted as a fact that prevention measures must work with. By shifting toward a prevention approach based on pattern of drinking, it is possible to distinguish between safe and hazardous behavior, between responsible and reckless drinking.

Thus, harm-reduction measures are neutral regarding the long-term goals of intervention. They do not exclude the possibility that the eventual goal of intervention might include abstention for individuals who cannot control alcohol intake. Indeed, in some instances, such as when they form part of a tertiary prevention package, harm-reduction measures can be a first step toward reducing or even ceasing alcohol use. Harm reduction involves a prioritization of goals, in which immediate and realizable goals take priority when dealing with reckless drinkers who cannot realistically be expected to cease drinking, but it need not conflict with an eventual goal of abstention, when such a goal is appropriate for a particular individual or group. It is, however, incompatible with a view that holds abstention to be the most appropriate goal for society at large, whether or not that goal is seen as attainable. It is simply neutral regarding the long-term goal of interventions, which are pragmatic rather than ideological in their orientation.

Thus, as the term is used in the following discussion, harm reduction refers to those measures that focus on decreasing the risk and severity of adverse consequences arising from alcohol consumption without necessarily decreasing the level of consumption. It is essentially a practical rather than an idealized approach: the standard of success is not some ideal drinking level or situation (abstention or low-risk levels) but whether or not the chances of adverse consequences have been reduced by the introduction of the prevention measure.

Promising Approaches to Harm Reduction

It may be helpful at this stage to give some examples of promising approaches to harm reduction in this field. It should be emphasized that this list is intended to be illustrative of the range of potential measures rather than a comprehensive account of available experience. It should also be emphasized that it is frequently by combining measures, particularly at a community level, that results are likely to be most encouraging.

• *Alcohol education.* Although some reviews of alcohol education have suggested that its capacity to initiate and sustain behavior change is less impressive than its proponents would like to suggest, there certainly have been promising examples, such as the French public education campaign (beginning with the *Bonjour les dégâts* television announcements) and the campaigns to reduce drunk driving in Australia and the United Kingdom. . . .

• *Responsible hospitality programs.* The development of server intervention programs represents a harm-reduction measure in several respects. Such programs develop house policies to promote moderation, for example, by quality upgrading and by avoiding discounts such as "happy hours" or house specials. Operators are encouraged to monitor entry to prevent underage or intoxicated persons from entering an establishment. Staff are trained to recognize signs of intoxication and gradually to cease service of alcohol to patrons approaching intoxication. Servers are also trained to manage intoxicated patrons appropriately (including the provision of safe transportation home) should these preventive efforts fail. Server intervention programs attempt thereby to reduce problems associated with drinking, particularly impaired driving, without restricting drinking by the majority of drinkers. Evaluation studies have generally shown that establishments that have undergone server intervention programming tend to attract more customers and to be more profitable.

Alcoholics Anonymous Does Not Help Prisoners

A 1997 survey conducted at the University of Georgia found that more than 90 percent of private treatment programs are based on AA's 12 steps [which are part of AA's abstinence treatment program]. Why, then, is our prison population at record levels, and why is so much of this crime associated with substance abuse? [Oklahoma governor Frank] Keating approvingly refers to a Department of Justice finding that most criminals are substance abusers, including a "staggering 83 percent of state inmates." Keating cites several studies that have found that inmates who complete treatment and continue to attend AA have better records than untreated prisoners and parolees. However, studies that include dropouts from treatment groups in their calculations have reported different results. For instance, a 1999 study of Texas' correctional substance abuse treatment programs found that those who participated in an in-prison program had the same recidivism rates as non-participants. Although those who completed the program did better than untreated offenders, those who entered but did not complete the program did worse. Moreover, probationers enrolled in treatment in Texas had an overall higher recidivism rate than non-participants.

Stanton Peele, *Reason*, May 2001.

• *Measures to encourage quality control of beverage alcohol.* Although such measures have special relevance for some developing countries, where there is an urgent need to test for methanol content or to identify toxic contaminants, they are also relevant to special situations in some industrialized countries. An excellent example is provided from Canada by the introduction of special early opening hours for a store of the Alberta Liquor Control Board in downtown Edmonton. The objective of the early opening was to reduce the use of potentially lethal nonbeverage alcohol by skid row inebriates. The measure was not intended to reduce their consumption; indeed, it was expected to increase their consumption of *potable* alcohol. It was focused exclusively on reducing adverse consequences from drinking substances such as shoe polish.

• *Measures designed to ameliorate adverse consequences of intoxication.* Rather than reducing the likelihood that intoxication will occur, these measures reduce the likelihood that serious damage will result. One of the best examples of such measures is the introduction in Scottish pubs of special glassware that crystallizes rather than shatters when broken, resulting in fewer injuries from accidents or if a fight breaks out. Other measures include changes in the physical structure of drinking establishments to minimize the risk of accidents or reduce the harm that may result if a fight occurs (e.g., padding of furniture and compartmentalization of space). The *Nez Rouge* (Red Nose) program in Quebec is a community-based service providing two volunteer drivers (one for the drinker and one for his or her vehicle) to anyone who has had too much to drink at a party or licensed establishment. There are also measures not specifically aimed at drinking problems, such as the introduction of seat belts and air bags in cars, which have reduced the risk and severity of adverse consequences from drinking.

• *Early identification and simple interventions.* The evidence that has accumulated on the efficacy and cost-effectiveness of simple screening procedures and brief interventions at the primary-care level is now considerable. Many such programs concentrate upon specific indicators of harm and have as their objective the modification of drinking patterns to avoid the persistence of the occurrence or risk of such harm. . . .

• *Controlled drinking programs.* Controlled drinking as a treatment alternative for persons with alcohol-related problems may also be considered a harm-reduction measure. As with other harm-reduction measures, focus is placed on reducing the risk and severity of problems resulting from drinking. Just as harm-reduction measures for illicit drug users do not preclude abstention as a long-term goal, controlled drinking programs do not preclude abstinence as a possible outcome for some drinkers. However, the immediate concern is to reduce the problems associated with drinking. The controversy over controlled drinking is similar in many ways to the acrimonious debate between harm-reduction and zero-tolerance approaches regarding illicit drugs.

Choice Need Not Be Restricted

As noted above, these examples are intended to be illustrative rather than comprehensive. . . . Nor should it be assumed that such measures constitute the totality of a comprehensive approach to the prevention of alcohol-related harm. The population approach to providing a balance between reasonable access and reasonable restrictions obviously creates the broad social context within which harm-reduction measures can be expected to be particularly effective. The difference is that the harm-reduction approach does not presume that the freedom of choice of the majority need be restricted in order to confer some protection, whether real or spurious, on a vulnerable or irresponsible minority.

"Of all the forms of drug treatment we have tried, methadone is by far the most effective."

Methadone Is the Most Effective Treatment for Heroin Addiction

Stephen Chapman

Methadone treatment is the best way for heroin addicts to conquer their drug dependency, Stephen Chapman claims in the following viewpoint. He argues that methadone has no serious side effects and does not pose a long-term health risk. Chapman asserts that the obstacles to methadone treatment, such as requiring addicts to go to a clinic every day to receive the medicine, should be lifted because heroin abuse will decrease if methadone is more readily available. Chapman is a syndicated columnist.

As you read, consider the following questions:

1. As stated by Chapman, how do junkies who turn to methadone improve their lives?
2. Why is methadone treatment more expensive than necessary, according to the author?
3. What has been the effect of legalizing methadone in Amsterdam, according to Chapman?

Stephen Chapman, "Resisting a Solution to the Drug Problem," *Conservative Chronicle*, August 12, 1998, p. 18. Copyright © 1998 by Creators Syndicate, Inc. Reproduced by permission.

Americans are endlessly searching for solutions to our drug problem. Beefing up law enforcement has cost a lot but accomplished little. Legalization is too scary. Education and "just say no" campaigns haven't gotten rid of the dealers or the addicts. Is there another answer?

It so happens there is, at least for the growing problem of heroin addiction, but it comes with a catch. This solution costs very little, reduces the crime and other social ills caused by drug use and doesn't involve legalization. What's the catch? The catch is that we have to be sensible for a change.

Methadone Works

The remedy is methadone, which has been used for nearly 30 years to relieve the symptoms of withdrawal from heroin addiction. Drug experts widely agree that of all the forms of drug treatment we have tried, methadone is by far the most effective.

Junkies who turn to methadone, studies have shown, improve their lives in all sorts of ways. They commit less crime. They reduce or eliminate their use of illegal drugs. They are less apt to contract the virus that causes AIDS. They pose less of a danger to themselves and everyone else.

Many patients have to stay on the drug indefinitely, but this is no cause for concern. At about $4,000 a year to participate in a treatment program, it's much cheaper than a heroin habit, which can cost 10 times that much. In the right dose, methadone doesn't produce a "high" or a sedative effect. Patients remain clear-headed, alert and able to carry on normal daily tasks, from working to driving. There are no significant side effects or long-term risks.

The downside? There is none. Skeptics lament the diversion of some methadone to the black market and disapprove of trading one form of opiate addiction for another.

But this is petty carping. Methadone is never going to be a big party drug. The only people likely to buy it are addicts who would otherwise buy heroin—possibly people who want to quit but can't or won't go to a clinic. How, exactly, does that worsen the drug problem?

True, it makes absolutely no sense to trade one addiction for another—unless, of course, you want to help junkies become rational, productive, law-abiding citizens whose drug "problem" is no worse than that of a depressed person on Prozac. Why should it bother us if reformed heroin addicts need a legal drug to stay clean? Isn't staying clean enough of an accomplishment?

Unfortunately, our national policy on methadone has been defined by its minor dangers, not its great promise. Ethan Nadelmann and Jennifer McNeely of the Lindesmith Center, a drug-policy think tank in New York, wrote in *The Public Interest*, "Methadone-maintenance patients—many of whom stay in treatment for 20 or 30 years—are often subject to stricter supervision than convicted probationers and parolees."

An addict who wants methadone treatment has to go to a special clinic that is staffed by doctors who have been specifically authorized to dispense the drugs, laboring under a welter of regulations on staffing, security, record-keeping and treatment. In some places, an addict has to go to the clinic every day to get her medicine, even if it means hours of driving. Regular urine tests are mandatory.

⌐Safe and Effective

Methadone's effects last for about 24 hours—four to six times as long as those of heroin—so people in treatment need to take it only once a day. Also, methadone is medically safe even when used continuously for 10 years or more. Combined with behavioral therapies or counseling and other supportive services, methadone enables patients to stop using heroin (and other opiates) and return to more stable and productive lives.

National Institute on Drug Abuse, "Heroin: Abuse and Addiction," 2002.

As a result, methadone treatment costs far more than it needs to, and many addicts give it up or never start it because of the hassle. A study issued [in 1997] by the National Academy of Sciences found that current policy "puts too much emphasis on protecting society from methadone and not enough on protecting society from the epidemics of addiction, violence and infectious diseases that methadone can help reduce."

Increased Accessibility

The best alternative is simple: Make methadone available by prescription, like other medicines, letting doctors dispense it to their patients who need it. Some addicts would continue to prefer clinics that provide counseling and job help. But, for the majority, whose only real need is methadone, the change would be a great boon.

Making methadone easier to get would almost certainly entice many heroin addicts to kick the habit. In Amsterdam, where methadone is much easier to get legally, the proportion of addicts in treatment is three times higher than in the United States.

Dr. Marc Shinderman, a psychiatrist who owns and runs the well-regarded Center for Addictive Problems in Chicago, argues that the medicine is now "severely over-regulated" and notes studies showing that addicts improve when they get no services but only methadone. "There would be some abuses with greater access, but they would be trivial compared to the benefits in terms of crime in the streets, illness and illicit drug use," he says.

Drug enforcers think we need even tighter controls. But they've got it backward. Methadone is a solution, not a problem. If we're not willing to embrace it, we should stop pretending that solutions are what we want.

Periodical Bibliography

The following articles have been selected to supplement the diverse views presented in this chapter.

Geoffrey Cowley	"New Ways to Stay Clean," *Newsweek*, February 12, 2001.
James L. Curtis	"Clean but Not Safe," *New York Times*, April 22, 1998.
Robert Fiorentine	"After Drug Treatment," *American Journal of Drug and Alcohol Abuse*, February 1999.
Michael J. Lemanski	"Addiction: Alternatives for Recovery," *Humanist*, January 2000.
Charles Levendosky	"Deceptive Drug Tests of Pregnant Women Unconstitutional," *Liberal Opinion Week*, June 11, 2001.
Joe Loconte	"Killing Them Softly," *Policy Review*, July/August 1998.
Michael Massing	"Winning the Drug War Isn't So Hard After All," *New York Times Magazine*, September 6, 1998.
Eileen Moon	"Pregnant, Hooked and Booked," *Professional Counselor*, October 1998.
Mark W. Parrino	"Methadone Treatment in Jail," *American Jails*, May/June 2000.
Stanton Peele	"Drunk With Power," *Reason*, May 2001.
Marsha Rosenbaum	"Women and Treatment," *Drug Policy Letter*, Winter 1998.
Sally Satel	"A Dangerous Place for Crack Moms?" *Women's Quarterly*, Spring 1999.
Maia Szalavitz	"Heroin Hassles," *Village Voice*, January 11, 2000.

CHAPTER 4

Should Drug Laws Be Reformed?

Chapter Preface

The war on drugs is not fought exclusively within the borders of the United States. The American government frequently focuses its efforts on nations such as Colombia, where much of the world's illegal drugs are produced. In July 2000, Congress authorized a $1.3 billion foreign aid package named "Plan Colombia." The funds went primarily toward military aid, including purchasing sixty attack helicopters, training Colombian soldiers, and establishing anti-drug operations throughout South America. Many critics of America's drug control policies contend that Plan Colombia has worsened the lives of Colombians.

One of the charges leveled against the plan is that it benefits a military that mistreats Colombia's citizenry. According to Sharon Fratepietro, writing for the *Humanist*, the Colombian army is beset by numerous human rights violations and is reportedly tied to drug trafficking. She argues "By supporting the Colombian military through Plan Colombia, the United States also supports the paramilitary death squads who serve as the vanguard of the Colombian army." James Petras, in an article for the *Monthly Review*, observes, "In its early stages, Plan Colombia has led to a more aggressive use of paramilitary forces and greater civilian casualties." The plan targets regions controlled by the Revolutionary Armed Forces of Colombia (FARC in its Spanish acronym) and the National Liberation Army (ELN), both of which are considered foreign terrorist organizations by the U.S. State Department.

Critics of the plan also maintain that spraying coca plants with herbicides—another element of Plan Colombia—has backfired. Fratepietro states that fumigation of coca plants has led to economic and environmental devastation and has also been linked to birth defects. Opponents of Plan Colombia point out that the herbicide damages nearby commercial crops such as coffee and bananas. In addition, thousands of Colombians have experienced skin problems, vomiting, and chemical poisoning after being exposed to the fumigant.

Plan Colombia is one example of the U.S. government's efforts to reduce the problem of chemical dependency. In the following chapter, the authors debate the effectiveness of several other approaches to lessening drug addiction in America.

"Drug-control programs are among the most successful public-policy efforts of the later half of the 20th century."

The War on Drugs Can Succeed

William J. Bennett

Despite the failures of the Clinton administration, the war on drugs can succeed, William J. Bennett contends in the following viewpoint. He argues that federal drug-control programs led to a significant decline in illegal drug use during the 1980s and early 1990s. However, Bennett notes, the nation's drug policy was neglected during Bill Clinton's presidency, when little support was given to the director of the Office of National Drug Control Policy. Bennett maintains that a renewed war on drugs—one that combines prevention campaigns and effective treatment programs—will meet with the success of earlier decades. Bennett is cochairman of the Partnership for a Drug-Free America and was the director of the Office of National Drug Control Policy under President George H.W. Bush.

As you read, consider the following questions:
1. How much did drug use fall between 1979 and 1992, as stated by Bennett?
2. In the author's opinion, what is the key to any antidrug strategy?
3. According to Bennett, what people will assist the new drug czar?

William J. Bennett, "The Bush Agenda," *Opinion Journal*, May 15, 2001.
Copyright © 2001 by *Opinion Journal*. Reproduced by permission.

George W. Bush announced the nomination of John P. Walters to serve as the director of the Office of National Drug Control Policy. The new "drug czar" is being asked to lead the nation's war on illegal drugs at a time when many are urging surrender.

The Drug War Has Not Failed

The forms of surrender are manifold: Buzzwords like "harm reduction" are crowding out clear no-use messages. State initiatives promoting "medical marijuana" are little more than thinly veiled legalization efforts (as underscored by [a May 2001] 8–0 Supreme Court ruling against medical exceptions). The film "Traffic" portrayed the war on drugs as a futile effort. In a survey by the Pew Research Center for the People and the Press, 74% of Americans believe the war on drugs is a failure.

And yet history shows that, far from being a failure, drug-control programs are among the most successful public-policy efforts of the later half of the 20th century. According to a national drug survey, between 1979 and 1992, the most intense period of antidrug efforts, the rate of illegal drug use dropped by more than half, while marijuana use decreased by two-thirds. Cocaine use dropped by three-fourths between 1985 and 1992.

Why is this record described as a failure? For those who would legalize drugs, all drug-control efforts must be painted as disastrous. But for most Americans, frustration with the drug issue stems from the fact that [since the early 1990s] we have lost ground.

The Neglect of the Clinton Administration

During the Clinton administration, our nation's drug policy suffered a period of malign neglect. President Bill Clinton's two clearest statements about illegal drugs were his infamous statement "I didn't inhale" and his immediate and dramatic cut in the size of the federal antidrug staff. Morale and political leadership were both compromised, and a national cynicism about drug use resulted. Hiring a four-star general may have fooled the public and the Washington press corps for a while, but it didn't add up to a meaningful program.

To paraphrase [playwright] Arthur Miller, attention was not paid, and the problem quickly worsened: Between 1992 and 1999, rates of current drug use—defined as using once a month or more—increased by 15%. Rates of marijuana use increased 11%. The situation was far worse among our children: Lifetime use of illegal drugs increased by 37% among eighth-graders and 55% among 10th-graders. We have reached the point where more than one-quarter of all high school seniors are current users of illegal drugs; indeed, rates of monthly drug use among high school seniors increased 86% between 1992 and 1999.

We must re-engage this fight. What we were doing in the 1980s and early 1990s—vigorous law enforcement and interdiction coupled with effective prevention and treatment—worked. It can work again.

Prevention and Treatment

The most important component of any antidrug strategy is prevention. Children who reach the age of 21 without using illegal drugs are almost certain never to do so. The Partnership for a Drug-Free America has crafted some of the most memorable and effective advertisements in history, encouraging children to turn down illegal drugs. The message that drug use is dangerous and immoral is the essential key to prevention.

In addition, we must continue to develop effective treatment programs. Many criticisms have been leveled at America's lack of treatment capacity, but more troubling is the lack of treatment efficacy. However, 12-step programs (akin to Alcoholics Anonymous) have been shown to be both inexpensive and effective in private-sector drug treatment. Hopefully, their success can be extended to public-sector treatment as well.

Everyone agrees on the necessity of effective treatment and strong prevention efforts. Some people, however, believe that law enforcement should have no role in the process. This is an altogether simplistic model: Demand reduction cannot be effective without supply reduction.

It is true that there will always be a supply of illegal drugs as long as there is a demand. But forceful interdiction can help

Federal Spending to Combat Drugs

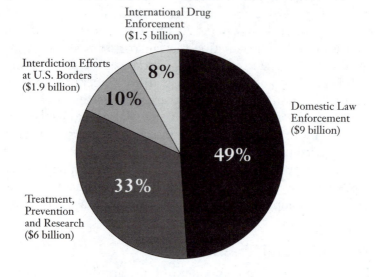

International Drug Enforcement ($1.5 billion)

Interdiction Efforts at U.S. Borders ($1.9 billion)

Domestic Law Enforcement ($9 billion)

Treatment, Prevention and Research ($6 billion)

8%

10%

49%

33%

Office of National Drug Control Policy, 2000.

to increase the price and decrease the purity of drugs available, a critical means of intervening in the lives of addicts, who can only beg, borrow and steal so much to support their habit. Government reports document that recovering addicts are more likely to relapse when faced with cheap, plentiful drugs. Aggressive interdiction efforts, then, are not supply reduction so much as the first step in demand reduction. Some people will admit that there is a place for law enforcement, but contend we spend too much on this effort, to the detriment of demand reduction. In fact, according to Robert DuPont, who led the nation's antidrug efforts under Presidents Richard Nixon and Gerald Ford, there has never been as much federal money spent on prevention education as is being spent today. The U.S.'s total spending on drug-demand reduction far exceeds the amounts spent in the rest of the world combined.

The Role of the Federal Government

A more pragmatic point: While treatment is often centered at the individual and local levels, interdiction and law enforcement must be federal responsibilities. Given the scope and complexity of drug trafficking, the federal government can and must assume the responsibility for stopping the traffic of drugs across and within our borders. The drug czar's first concerns, then, must be interdiction and law enforcement, if only because they are tasks no other agency can perform as effectively.

I believe that the position of drug czar ought to remain at the cabinet level, but more important is the president's personal support and commitment to the office. I had that backing, and I expect the new drug czar will enjoy that same support and commitment from Mr. Bush. If Mr. Walters is to have any success, he must enjoy it.

The past eight years are, once again, illustrative: General Barry McCaffrey never enjoyed that support from President Clinton. In renewing the drug war, the new drug czar will not be alone. He will be able to draw on the assistance of people—parents, teachers, substance-abuse counselors, clergymen and elected officials—who have continued to fight drug use [since 1993]. These groups are our first lines of defense; without them, the regression since 1992 would have been far worse. Their dedication gives the lie to the gospel of futility.

I look forward to America re-engaging in the war on drugs—and continuing the success that we had between 1980 and 1992.

"Drug policy in America needs to be reinvented."

The War on Drugs Has Failed

Timothy Lynch

In the following article, Timothy Lynch asserts that America's war on drugs has been an expensive failure. According to Lynch, although the United States has spent billions of dollars since Richard Nixon created the Drug Enforcement Administration in 1973, millions of Americans continue to use drugs and the flow of drugs into the country has not been reduced. In addition, Lynch argues that the war on drugs has resulted in a mammoth criminal-justice system and a number of troubling police practices. He concludes that America must reinvent its drug policy. Lynch is the director of the Cato Institute's Project on Criminal Justice and the editor of the book *After Prohibition: An Adult Approach to Drug Policies in the 21st Century.*

As you read, consider the following questions:
1. In Lynch's opinion, why do supporters of the drug war consider drug use immoral?
2. According to a *New York Times* article cited by the author, how frequently do drug arrests occur in the United States?
3. What are some of the "undesirable police practices" used in the war on drugs, according to Lynch?

Timothy Lynch, *After Prohibition*. Washington, DC: The Cato Institute, 2000. Copyright © 2000 by The Cato Institute. Reproduced by permission.

A merica's drug policies are never seriously debated in Washington. Year after year, our elected representatives focus on two questions: How much more money should we spend on the drug war? and, How should it be spent? In the months preceding elections, politicians typically try to pin blame for the drug problem on one another.

After the election, the cycle begins anew.

A Growing Dissatisfaction

Outside the capital, however, there is growing unease about the war on drugs. More and more Americans are concluding that the drug war has been given a chance to work—and has failed. Voters in California, Arizona, Oregon, Washington, Nevada, Alaska, and Maine have rejected the lobbying efforts of federal officials and approved initiatives calling for the legalization of marijuana for medicinal purposes. Two sitting governors, Jesse Ventura of Minnesota and Gary Johnson of New Mexico, have declared the drug war a failure. As public opinion continues to turn against the war, we can expect more elected officials to speak out.

Federal officials do not yet appreciate the extent of public dissatisfaction with the war on drugs. Congress continues to propose and enact laws with such platitudinous titles as "The Drug-Free Century Act." Not many people outside the capital are even paying attention to those laws, and even fewer take the rhetoric seriously.

To be sure, some people of good will continue to support the drug war. Their rationale is that we may not be close to achieving a "drug-free" society, but our present situation would only deteriorate if the government were to stop prosecuting the drug war. The burden of persuasion on that proposition has always rested with drug reformers. But nowadays it is a burden reformers happily accept, buoyed as they are by the realization that momentum in the debate is shifting in their direction.

The Arguments of Drug War Advocates

Reformers are as eager as ever to debate the efficacy of the drug laws, while supporters of the drug war discuss the issue only grudgingly. Reformers ask: Why should an adult man or woman be arrested, prosecuted, and imprisoned for using heroin, opium, cocaine, or marijuana? The answer, according to the most prominent supporters of the drug war, is simple: Drug use is wrong. It is wrong because it is immoral, and it is immoral because it degrades human beings. The prominent social scientist James Q. Wilson has articulated that view as follows: "Even now, when the dangers of drug use are well understood, many educated people still discuss the drug problem in almost every way except the right way. They talk about the 'costs' of drug use and the 'socioeconomic factors' that shape that use. They rarely speak plainly—drug use is wrong because it is immoral and it is immoral because it enslaves the mind and destroys the soul."

William J. Bennett, America's first drug czar, has expressed a similar view: "A citizen in a drug-induced haze, whether on his backyard deck or on a mattress in a ghetto crack house, is not what the Founding Fathers meant by the 'pursuit of happiness.'. . . Helpless wrecks in treatment centers, men chained by their noses to cocaine—these people are slaves."

Wilson, Bennett, and their supporters believe that to eradicate this form of slavery, the government should vigorously investigate, prosecute, and jail anyone who sells, uses, or possesses mind-altering drugs. The criminal sanction should be used—in Bennett's words—"to take drug users off the streets and deter new users from becoming more deeply involved in so hazardous an activity."

For more than 25 years, the political establishment has offered unflagging support for the ban on drugs. In 1973, President Richard Nixon created the Drug Enforcement Administration, a police agency that focuses exclusively on federal drug-law violations. President Ronald Reagan designated narcotics an official threat to America's national security; he also signed legislation authorizing the military to assist federal and state police agencies in the drug war. In 1988, Congress created the Office of National Drug Control Policy; President George Bush Sr. appointed Bennett national drug czar to centralize control and coordinate activities of federal agencies in the drug war. President Bill Clinton appointed a former military commander, General Barry McCaffrey, as drug czar.

The Results of Drug-War Efforts

Since the early 1970s, Congress has been escalating the federal government's drug-war efforts. In 1979, the federal government spent $900 million on various antidrug programs; in 1989, it spent $5 billion; by 1999, it was spending nearly $18 billion.

According to the Office of National Drug Control Policy, vigorous law-enforcement tactics help reduce drug abuse chiefly by reducing demand and disrupting supply. Enforcement of the drug laws reduces demand by increasing social disapproval of substance abuse; arrest and threatened imprisonment also offer a powerful incentive for addicts to take treatment seriously. Drug enforcement disrupts supply by detecting and dismantling drug rings, which facilitate the movement of drugs from suppliers to the streets.

Bateman. © 2000 by Scott Bateman. Reprinted with permission of Kings Features Syndicate.

Congress has devoted billions of dollars to these tasks, and there have been palpable results. To begin with, the criminal-justice system has grown much larger: There are more police officers, prosecutors, judges, and prison guards than ever before. The number of arrests, convictions, and prisoners has increased exponentially; so has the amount of seized contraband. In February 1999, the *New York Times* reported that "every 20 seconds, someone in America is arrested for a drug violation. Every week, on average, a new jail or prison is built to lock up more people in the world's largest penal system."

There is certainly a lot of government activity; but is the Office of National Drug Control Policy really achieving its twin objectives of reducing demand and disrupting supply? The demand for illegal drugs remains strong. According to the National Household Survey on Drug Abuse, 11 million Americans can be classified as "current users" (past month) of marijuana and 1.75 million Americans as current users of cocaine. As startling as those numbers are, they represent only the tip of the proverbial iceberg. Millions of other individuals can be classified as "occasional users," and tens of thousands of people use less popular illicit drugs, such as heroin and methamphetamine. In short: The government's own statistics admit that millions and millions of Americans break the law every single month.

The Drug Supply Has Not Decreased

The supply of drugs has not been hampered in any serious way by the war on drugs. A commission on federal law-enforcement practices chaired by former FBI director William Webster recently offered this blunt assessment of the interdiction efforts: "Despite a record number of seizures and a flood of legislation, the Commission is not aware of any evidence that the flow of narcotics into the United States has been reduced." Perhaps the most dramatic evidence of the failure of the drug war is the flourishing of open-air drug markets in Washington, D.C.—the very city in which the drug czar and the Drug Enforcement Administration have their headquarters.

Even though law enforcement has been unable to seriously disrupt either the supply of or the demand for illegal drugs, many hesitate to draw the conclusion that the drug war has failed. They choose to focus on the evils of drug use, and the need to keep up the fight against it, on the grounds that even an incomplete success is better than a surrender. But a fair appraisal of the drug war must look beyond drug use itself, and take into account all of the negative repercussions of the drug war. It is undeniable that the criminalization of drug use has created an immense and sophisticated black market that generates billions of dollars for gangster organizations. The criminal proceeds are often used to finance other criminal activity. Furthermore, rival gangs use violence to usurp and defend territory for drug sales. Innocent people die in the crossfire.

Then there is the cost. Billions of taxpayer dollars are squandered every year to keep drugs from entering the country. The government cannot even keep narcotics out of its own prisons—and yet it spends millions every month trying to keep contraband from arriving by air, land, and sea.

Prosecuting the war also involves a disturbingly large number of undesirable police practices: Paramilitary raids, roadblocks, wiretaps, informants, and property seizures have all become routine because of the difficulty of detecting drug offenses. Countless innocent people have had their phones tapped and their homes and cars searched. A criminal-justice system that devotes its limited resources to drug offenders is necessarily distracted from investigating other criminal activity—such as murder, rape, and theft.

An Alternative to Drug Prohibition

Unfortunately, the most prominent supporters of the drug war have refused to grapple with these grim consequences of their policy. Drug legalization, they retort, would undermine the moral sanction against drug use. William Bennett has actually indulged in a comparison that would equate alternative drug policies—such as decriminalization—with surrender to the Nazis: "Imagine if, in the darkest days of 1940, Winston Churchill had rallied the West by saying, 'This war looks hopeless, and besides, it will cost too much. [Adolf] Hitler can't be that bad. Let's surrender and see what happens.' That is essentially what we hear from the legalizers." After decades of ceaseless police work, it is safe to say that Bennett is confusing perseverance with bullheadedness. One thoughtful analyst, Father John Clifton Marquis, recognized—as long ago as 1990—that "when law does not promote the common good, but in fact causes it to deteriorate, the law itself becomes bad and must be changed. . . . Authentic moral leaders cannot afford the arrogant luxury of machismo, with its refusal to consider not 'winning.'" Marquis is correct; and this is precisely why Bennett's World War II imagery is misplaced. The notion that the drug czar is somehow leading an army against an evil foe is an example of what Marquis calls "arrogant machismo." A more apt analogy would be America's 15-year experience with alcohol prohibition: Americans rejected Prohibition because experience showed the federal liquor laws to be unenforceable and because alcohol prohibition led to gang wars and widespread corruption. The war on drugs has created a similar set of problems.

The most valuable lesson that can be drawn from the Prohibition experience is that government cannot effectively engineer social arrangements. Policymakers simply cannot repeal the economic laws of supply and demand. Nor can they foresee the unintended consequences that follow government intervention. Students of American history will someday wonder how today's lawmakers could readily admit that alcohol prohibition was a disastrous mistake, but simultaneously engage in a reckless policy of drug prohibition.

Drug policy in America needs to be reinvented, starting with a tabula rasa. Policymakers ought to address the issue in an open, honest, and mature manner. A growing number of Americans are coming to the conclusion that the law should treat substances such as marijuana and cocaine the same way it treats tobacco, beer, and whiskey: restricting sales to minors and jailing any user who endangers the safety of others (by, for example, operating an automobile while under the influence). Education, moral suasion, and noncoercive social pressure are the only appropriate ways to discourage adult drug use in a free and civil society.

"No one should be arrested if their only crime is putting certain chemicals into their bloodstream."

Drug Use Should Be Decriminalized

Joseph D. McNamara

In the following viewpoint, Joseph D. McNamara claims that due to the problems associated with drug prohibition, marijuana should be decriminalized and that no one should be arrested for using drugs that are currently illegal, as long as no other crime has been committed. He argues that drug prohibition is flawed because drug laws typically target minorities, are associated with unlawful searches and perjury by police officers, and do not lessen drug use. He concludes that the United States should follow the lead of nations such as Switzerland and the Netherlands, both of which have lowered crime rates by regulating drug use. McNamara is a retired police chief and a research fellow at the Hoover Institution, an organization that supports private enterprise and a limited federal government.

As you read, consider the following questions:

1. What percentage of illegal drug shipments to the United States arrives undetected?
2. Why does the author criticize the jailing of drug users?
3. According to McNamara, how many arrests would be eliminated annually if marijuana were decriminalized?

Joseph D. McNamara, "Drug Peace—Legalization Research: The New Millennium," *Vital Speeches of the Day*, vol. 66, November 1, 1999, p. 39.
Copyright © 1999 by Joseph D. McNamara. Reproduced by permission.

The federal budget for the drug war in the first year of the new millennium is $17.8 billion. In 1972, when President Richard Nixon called for a war against drugs, the federal drug war budget was roughly $101 million.

Increased Federal Spending

United States drug control policies evoke considerable differences of opinion. Yet there is consensus that America's drug problems have not been resolved despite enormous increases in government efforts. One indicator of the difficulties inherent in preventing illegal drug use is in the growth of federal spending on drug control.

The magnitude of the increase can be seen by comparing the average 1972 monthly social security payment of $177 with the growth of drug control spending. If social security benefits had increased at the same rate, current monthly social security payments would be $30,444 rather than [2001's] $900.

Similarly, the average 1972 weekly salary of $114 would have soared to $19,608, and a mortgage payment of $408 would have grown to $68,000 a month. It is noteworthy that these comparisons take into account only federal spending. If state and local drug control expenditures are considered, the total cost estimates are approximately $40 billion a year, more than double the federal costs.

Despite this growing expenditure of taxpayers' money, this decade has seen a doubling of opium production in Southeast Asia and an increase of cocaine production by one third in Central and South America, 80–90% of illegal drugs shipped to this country arrive undetected. Eleven years after Congress proclaimed: "It is the declared policy of the United States to create a Drug-Free America by 1995." The United States, indeed the world, is awash in illegal drugs that are purer and more potent than ever.

The Drug Problem Continues

The vast profits resulting from prohibition—a markup as great as 17,000%—have led to worldwide corruption of public officials and widespread violence among drug traffickers and dealers that endanger whole communities, cities, and nations. The United Nations reports that there is a $500 billion international black market in drugs. In our own country, drug-related overdose deaths and emergency room visits have increased. Half of all high school seniors surveyed report using an illegal drug and 85% of them say illegal drugs are easier to obtain than beer.

President Bill Clinton assures us we are winning against drugs, as did his predecessors. Yet people in law enforcement and local communities are unconvinced, and for good reason. Although it appears that casual illegal drug use has declined in recent years, regular use has not. More young people are using drugs and starting use at an earlier age.

Furthermore, the decline in casual drug use may be unrelated to the war on drugs. Cigarette smoking, and consumption of hard liquor and high cholesterol food, all as dangerous as illegal drug use, declined because of greater awareness of health dangers, not because consumers were jailed or because the government reduced the supply of these substances.

As we approach the year 2000, we should be mindful that the drug war started roughly 100 years ago.

The Social Damage of Drug Prohibition

Protestant missionaries in China and other religious groups joined with temperance organizations in convincing Congress that drugs were evil and that drug users were dangerous, immoral people. On December 17, 1914, the religious groups got their version of sin outlawed in the Harrison Act. Until this federal law, the nation had viewed drug use as a social and medical dilemma. Making possession of drugs a federal crime was a radical change in policy. It certainly did not solve the drug problem but it did give birth to unanticipated social damage.

I was a policeman for thirty-five years of [the twentieth] century. As a beat officer in New York's Harlem, and as police chief in Kansas City and San Jose, I caused many drug users to be locked up. I have come to believe that jailing people simply because they put certain chemicals into their bloodstream is a gross misuse of the police and criminal law. Jailing drug users does not lessen drug use, and incarceration usually destroys the person's life and does immense harm to their families and neighborhoods. And justifying jail sentences by claiming that users would likely commit other crimes if they remained free is a flagrant rejection of a fundamental American right—the presumption of innocence.

Destroying the Black Market

Any solution [to the drug problem] that leaves gangsters in control of the market will not cure the cancer, and no matter what short-range problems may be solved, the corruption will only be fertilized. The only way to destroy the black market is to underbid it. If that means drugs have to be given away to serious addicts, so be it. Anyone who's determined to use heroin regardless of the consequences must be able to get the stuff from a legitimate source at a price that doesn't require stealing car radios. A tightly controlled legal market, offering clean, unadulterated pharmaceuticals, would instantly terminate the cash flow to the street bazaar, and the river of money that has fueled the most brutal collection of criminal combines in the history of the planet would dry up like a Mojave arroyo on Independence Day.

Mike Gray, *Drug Crazy*, 1998.

Non-whites have borne the brunt of the punishment even though most drug use is by whites. Alfred Blumstein, former president of the American Society of Criminologists, described the drug war as "an assault on the African American community." The current protests over racial profiling by the police are a reflection of the damage that an ill-conceived law enforcement war against drugs has on the ability of the police to win the cooperation that they need to do their job.

Troubling Police Behavior

Because drug transactions are consensual, the police do not have a victim, witnesses, and physical evidence that help them solve crimes like murder, assault, robbery, rape and burglary. And under the Fourth Amendment, the police, with few exceptions, are not allowed to search people or their homes without a warrant. Yet, [in 1998] state and local police in the United States made approximately 1,400,000 arrests for illegal possession of drugs. Overwhelmingly, these were minor arrests and rarely involved a court-approved warrant.

The inescapable conclusion is that in hundreds of thousands of cases, police officers violated their oath to uphold the Constitution and often committed perjury so that the evidence would be admitted. The practice is so prevalent that the term "testilying" is often substituted in police jargon for "testifying." The injury that unlawful searches and perjury by the police does to the credibility of our justice system is immeasurable.

Just as damaging is the destruction of trust that follows exposure of gangster cops who have robbed drug dealers, sold drugs, and framed people in the communities that they were sworn to protect. Police perjurers by far outnumber those cops who are predatory drug criminals; still, there have been thousands of drug-related police crimes since the 1972 declaration of a drug war.

Treatment Instead of Arrests

The nation has been unable to face the failure of our drug policies and to examine alternatives that would lessen dangerous drug use. We are still captive to the myths about drug use and the false stereotypes of drug users created a century ago by religious zealots.

The new millennium provides the opportunity for reflection and change. Marijuana should be decriminalized. There is no record of anyone dying from marijuana or committing a murder under its effects. Any number of scientific studies have indicated that in some cases it may be an effective medicine. We would eliminate almost 700,000 arrests a year, which would save money and ruin fewer lives.

In addition, our country should revert to the pre–Harrison Act principle that no one should be arrested if their only crime is putting certain chemicals into their bloodstream. Treatment should be substituted for arrests. As to the "harder" drugs, we should reject the inane demagogic slogan "a drug-free America," accept that drugs will never be eradicated from our society, and recognize that users should be dealt with justly and humanely.

Once we are beyond the emotional straightjackets imposed by the Harrison Act lobbyists, we can study how other countries minimize the harm of drugs. The Swiss, for example, found during a five-year experiment that providing heroin to addicts actually reduced heroin use and significantly reduced the crime committed by the addicts. The Netherlands regulates and controls the distribution of small amounts of hashish and marijuana and has a lower per capita use of drugs and lower crime rates than the United States.

There is no panacea, but it is clear that continuing to do more of what has not worked in the past century is not the way to start a new millennium.

"If drugs were legalized, the cost to the individual and society would grow astronomically."

Drug Use Should Not Be Decriminalized

Barry McCaffrey

Decriminalizing drug use would have serious consequences, Barry McCaffrey asserts in the following viewpoint. According to McCaffrey, drug use is associated with higher rates of violence and child abuse, and increasing the availability of drugs would exacerbate such problems. In addition, he argues, addicts would be less likely to receive treatment if drugs were no longer illegal. McCaffrey concludes that the United States should not encourage risky and self-destructive behavior by legalizing drugs. McCaffrey was the director of the Office of National Drug Control Policy during President Bill Clinton's administration.

As you read, consider the following questions:
1. According to McCaffrey, how many deaths do illegal drugs cause each year in the United States?
2. In the author's opinion, what is the central question in the debate over legalization?
3. What other laws besides drug laws prohibit self-destructive behavior, as explained by McCaffrey?

Barry McCaffrey, "We Have No 'War on Drugs,'" *World & I*, vol. 15, February 2000, pp. 30–33. Copyright © 2000 by *World & I*. Reproduced by permission.

The ill-chosen term war on drugs illustrates the problem that can develop from using misplaced military metaphors. The so-called war on drugs is not the "longest war in U.S. history," as some have claimed, because the effort to reduce substance abuse is not a war. If we use the term war for any sustained initiative, we could term education the "war on ignorance." Then we might argue erroneously that since American schools failed to stamp out ignorance despite centuries of schooling, the country has lost what is truly the longest "war" and therefore should close all schools.

In fact, the United States is a lot closer to reducing substance abuse. Drug use among adults is down nearly 50 percent from its high point in the late 1970s. We have been winning with Americans who are mature enough to make sound, informed decisions. The recent decrease (13 percent in [1999]) in illegal drug use by teens shows that we are on the right track in our efforts to educate upcoming generations to avoid the dangers of addictive drugs.

The Dangers of Drug Abuse

Although the struggle to reduce drug use is not a war, illegal drugs contribute to the deaths of more than 50,000 Americans each year—close to the number of U.S. casualties during the entire Vietnam War. People who say that drug use is a victimless crime are ignoring the facts. Drug abuse imposes an unacceptable risk of harm on others. The evidence supporting this viewpoint is chilling:

• One study revealed that nondrug users who live in households where drugs are used are 11 times more likely to be killed than individuals from drug-free households. Drug abuse in the home renders a woman 28 times more likely to be killed by a close relative (*Journal of the American Medical Association*).

• More than half the crime in this country is committed by individuals under the influence of drugs. The majority of these crimes result from the effects of the drug, not from the fact that drugs are illegal. A study of drug-related homicides in New York found that 60 percent resulted from the psychopharmacological effects of illegal drugs ("Substance Abuse in Urban America: Its Impact on an American City," a Center on Addiction and Substance Abuse study).

• A survey of state child-welfare agencies identified substance abuse as one of the top two problems exhibited by 81 percent of families reported for child maltreatment. Researchers estimate that substance abuse is present in at least half of all child-abuse and neglect cases (National Committee to Prevent Child Abuse, DUF—Drug Use Forecasting, National Institute of Justice).

• Research from the National Institute on Drug Abuse shows that untreated opiate addicts die at a rate seven to eight times higher than similar patients in methadone-based treatment programs (Joe Loconte, "Killing Them Softly," *Policy Review*). Dr. James Curtis, director of addiction services at Harlem Hospital Center, explains: "It is false, misleading, and unethical to give addicts the idea that they can be intravenous drug abusers without suffering serious self-injury." Eighty-two percent of drug addicts die of causes other than AIDS, such as drug overdoses (Dr. G.W. Woody, *New England Journal of Medicine*). Intravenous drug users

---

The Dangers of Marijuana

Roughly 100,000 people are in rehab programs for marijuana use. The drug lobby claims most of them were arrested for possession and given the alternative of treatment or imprisonment.

That almost sounds plausible, until one looks at marijuana mentions in emergency-room visits. In 1999, more ER visits were related to marijuana than heroin (38,976 versus 38,237), though less than half that for cocaine, according to the University of Maryland Center for Substance Abuse Research. Of the marijuana cases, 27 percent had unexpected reactions, 18 percent had overdosed (something proponents assure us is impossible) and 14 percent sought detox.

Marijuana use alters personality in unpleasant ways. Based on data collected from 1994 to 1996, the center found a direct correlation between frequency of marijuana use and "delinquent/depressive behaviors." Among those ages 12 to 17 who had been placed on probation in the last year, 1 percent never used the drug, 7 percent used it one to 11 times during the year and 20 percent used it at least weekly.

Don Feder, *Insight on the News*, October 1, 2001.

---

contract septicemia, wounds botulism, and other severe conditions resulting from their drug habits.

Drugs themselves harm users. A significant percentage of users become addicted. Addiction is a brain disease that results from the introduction of foreign substances into the body which in turn change a person's neurochemistry. For four million chronically addicted Americans, drug use is not a choice; it has nothing to do with personal liberty. Sanctions on drug use, when combined with increased drug treatment resources, are the best hope many addicts have of regaining control of their lives. Compelling scientific evidence indicates that a large number of drug-dependent individuals will only complete treatment if forced to do so by the threat of criminal sanctions. A study of a Brooklyn forced-treatment program found that the percentage of offenders who stay in drug treatment is two to four times higher than for general residential treatment. Removing the threat of criminal sanctions eliminates the possibility of forced treatment, condemning addicts to miserable lives.

Arguing Against Legalization

One argument given for drug legalization by harm-reduction advocates is that the alleged "war" against drugs has been lost. This false line of reasoning ignores the fact that drug use in this country declined by half in the last two decades. The number of current users dropped from 25 million in 1979 to 13 million in 1996, while the number of current cocaine users plummeted from 5.7 million in 1985 to 1.75 million in 1998—a 69 percent decline.

Nevertheless, the execution of drug-control policy can still be improved. The National Drug Control Strategy is implementing important changes. The strategy's No. 1 goal is prevention. In the past four years, the administration increased spending on prevention by 55 percent, and over the past five years the investment in treatment rose 26 percent. The strategy calls for more treatment in the criminal justice system as well as scientific research to break the cycle of drugs, addiction, and crime. (The federal government's National Institute on Drug Abuse conducts 85 percent of the world's research on addiction.)

Fundamentally, the debate over drug legalization boils down to a question of risk. Studies show that the more a product is available and legitimized, the greater will be its use. If drugs were legalized, the cost to the individual and society would grow astronomically. Removing the criminal status associated with drug use and sale ultimately would produce more wrecked young lives.

Do Not Condone Self-Destruction

On a judicial level, the question of drug legalization comes down to whether we should condone destructive behavior. American jurisprudence has gone in the opposite direction for the individual and society at large. Americans have decided that people do not have a right to ride motorcycles without wearing helmets, drive cars without using seat belts, pollute the environment at will, or endanger themselves and others by refusing vaccination or similar lifesaving health measures. In general, our laws indicate that self-destructive activity should not be permitted. Drug consumption damages the brain, which in turn produces other forms of negative behavior. U.S. law does not grant people the right to destroy themselves or others. Addictive drugs were criminalized because they are harmful; they are not harmful because they were criminalized.

*"Mandatory minimum sentences put steel
in the spine of our criminal justice system."*

Mandatory Minimum Sentences Are Essential to the War on Drugs

David Risley

In the following viewpoint, David Risley contends that mandatory minimum sentences help discourage drug dealers. He argues that federal sentencing guidelines, which determine sentences based on the seriousness of the offense and the defendant's criminal record, should not take the place of mandatory minimums. According to Risley, the federal guidelines are too lenient toward marijuana growers. He asserts that Congress's mandatory minimum sentences more appropriately punish marijuana possession and use. Risley is an assistant district attorney in Illinois.

As you read, consider the following questions:

1. According to the author, how is the seriousness of a drug case determined?
2. How much marijuana does the typical cultivated marijuana plant produce?
3. As stated by Risley, what is the minimum sentence for producing between $26,400 and $120,000 worth of marijuana?

David Risley, "Mandatory Minimum Sentences: An Overview," www.drugwatch. org, May 2000. Copyright © 2000 by Drug Watch International. Reproduced by permission.

D rug dealers are risk takers by nature. Lack of certainty of serious sentences for serious crimes encourages, rather than deters, such risk takers to elevate their level of criminal activity in the hope that, if caught, they will be lucky enough to draw a lenient judge and receive a lenient sentence. The only possible deterrence for people who are willing to take extreme risks is to take away their cause for such hope.

A Business and a Crime

Some counter that drug dealers are undeterrable by criminal sanctions because they sell drugs to support their own addictions, and so should be treated for their addictions rather than imprisoned. While there may be some merit to that argument for many low-level street dealers, it is generally untrue of their suppliers, and even many other street dealers. Most dealers and distributors at any substantial level do not use drugs themselves, or do so only infrequently. They are exploiters and predators, and users are their captive prey. Drug dealing is a business. As in any other business, drug addicts are unreliable and untrustworthy, especially around drugs, and so make poor business partners. Because drug dealers usually run their operations as high-risk businesses, they necessarily weigh those risks carefully, and so are deterrable when the risks become too high. Many dealers who used to carry firearms, for example, now avoid doing so when they are selling drugs due to the high mandatory federal penalties when guns and drugs are mixed.

However, drug dealers seldom view the risks as too high when they see reason to hope for a light sentence. Congress, however, can, and did, step in to take away that hope. By establishing mandatory minimum sentences for serious drug offenses, Congress sent a clear message to drug dealers: no matter who the judge is, serious crime will get you serious time.

To those who do not view crimes subject to mandatory minimum sentences as serious, including drug dealers and their support systems, that message is objectionable. To most, it is welcome. Mandatory minimum sentences put steel in the spine of our criminal justice system. . . .

Understanding the Sentencing Guideline System

[One] question is whether the more recent advent of the federal sentencing guidelines, which also limit judicial sentencing discretion, made mandatory minimum penalties obsolete. The answer is definitely no. As a practical matter, only through mandatory minimum sentences can Congress maintain sentencing benchmarks for serious drug crimes which cannot be completely circumvented by the commission which establishes, and sometimes quietly alters, those guidelines. One of the best illustrations is that of the sentencing guidelines for marijuana growers, who have achieved favorable treatment under the sentencing guidelines, but fortunately not under Congress' statutory mandatory minimum sentences.

To appreciate the significance of that illustration, one must understand a little about the sentencing guideline system, and its relationship to mandatory minimum sentences. As part of the Sentencing Reform Act of 1984, Congress mandated the formation of the United States Sentencing Commission as an independent agency in the judicial branch composed of seven voting members, appointed by the President with the advice and consent of the Senate, at least three of whom must be federal judges, not more than four of whom may be from the same political party, serving staggered six-year terms. That Commission was charged with the formidable task of establishing binding sentencing guidelines to dramatically narrow judges' sentencing discretion, in order to provide reasonable uniformity in sentencing throughout the country, while at the same time taking into reasonable account the myriad of differences between the hundreds of federal crimes and limitless array of individual defendants.

The result of that enormous undertaking was the adoption, effective November 1987, of the United States Sentencing Guidelines. Using its provisions, contained in a book one inch thick, courts determine the seriousness of the offense and the extent of the defendant's past criminal history, and use that information to determine on a chart the relatively narrow sentencing range within which they have sentencing discretion. In drug cases, the seriousness of the offense (offense level) is determined mostly on the basis of the amount of drugs for which a defendant is accountable, with adjustments for factors such as role in the offense, whether a firearm was involved, and whether the defendant accepted responsibility for his or her actions through a candid guilty plea.

As part of its broad delegation of authority, Congress provided that changes promulgated by the Commission to the Sentencing Guidelines automatically become law unless Congress, within a 180-day waiting period, affirmatively acts to reject them. By that means Congress avoided a great deal of detailed work, but also created the possibility that changes to the Sentencing Guidelines to which they would object if carefully considered would become law if no one raises a sufficient alarm.

Because the Commission has only seven voting members, a change of only one member can result in the reversal of a previous 4–3 vote, sometimes with great consequences. Congress is ill-equipped to deal with the intricacies of the impact of many amendments to the Sentencing Guidelines, and is sometimes preoccupied with other, more pressing or "hot button" issues. Therefore, the only realistic check on the delegation of authority to the Commission to make changes in drug sentences is the trump card of mandatory minimums.

That is true because defendants receive the higher of whatever sentence is called for by the statutory mandatory minimums or the Sentencing Guidelines. If the Commission promulgates a change to the Sentencing Guidelines which calls for lower sentences than required by the statutory mandatory minimums, the mandatory minimums trump the Sentencing Guidelines. In other words, the mandatory minimums are mandatory, and are beyond the control of the Commission.

Marijuana and Mandatory Minimums

With that background, the vital importance of mandatory minimum sentences as at least a partial check over the Commission in drug sentences is dramatically illustrated by the changes the Commission made regarding sentences for marijuana growers. The mandatory minimum sentences for marijuana growers imposed by Congress, which kick in at 100 plants, equate one marijuana plant with one kilogram (2.2 pounds) of marijuana. Until November 1995, the Sentencing Guidelines used that same equivalency in calculating the offense level in cases involving 50 or more plants, but for cases involving less than 50 plants considered one plant as the equivalent of only 100 grams (3.5 ounces). That 10:1 ratio between the amount of marijuana which plants were considered to represent was a major logical inconsistency, since marijuana plants do not produce significantly more or less marijuana just because they happen to be in the company of more or less than 49 other marijuana plants.

Logical and Desirable

I do believe the mandatory minimum sentences for drug dealers are logical and desirable and that mandatory sentences, in my view, ought to be increased, especially for those who sell drugs to children, so that they serve even longer sentences in those situations.

Now mandatory minimum sentences, as a general rule, reflect the desires of people in a State or in America in the sense that it comes from Washington, and it is their sense of outrage over certain crimes.

George Allen, testimony before Congress, May 11, 2000.

The Commission solved that inconsistency in early 1995 by promulgating an amendment to the Sentencing Guidelines which, instead of eliminating the unrealistically low 100 gram equivalency for smaller cases, eliminated the one kilogram equivalency for larger cases. Congress did nothing, so, as of November 1995, the Sentencing Guidelines treat all marijuana plants as if they were only capable of producing 3.5 ounces of marijuana.

In actuality, a marijuana plant does not produce a yield of one kilogram of marijuana. The one plant = 100 grams of marijuana equivalency used by the Commission for offenses involving fewer than 50 marijuana plants was selected as a reasonable approximation of the actual average yield of marijuana plants taking into account (1) studies reporting the actual yield of marijuana plants (37.5 to 412 grams depending on growing conditions); (2) that all plants regardless of size are counted for guideline purposes while, in actuality, not all plants will produce useable marijuana (e.g., some plants may die of disease before maturity, and when plants are grown outdoors some plants may be consumed by animals); and (3) that male plants, which are counted for guideline purposes, are frequently culled because they do not produce the same quality marijuana as do female plants. To enhance fairness and consistency, this amendment adopts the equivalency of 100 grams per marijuana plant for all guideline determinations.

Contrary to those claims, no self-respecting commercial marijuana grower would ever admit his plants produce no more than 412 grams (14.5 ounces) of marijuana, much less that they average only 100 grams. Based upon long experience with actual marijuana growing operations, it is widely accepted in law enforcement circles that cultivated marijuana plants typically produce about one pound of marijuana (453 grams), and sometimes two pounds (907 grams). While it is true that some growers cull out the male plants in order to produce the potent form of marijuana known as sinsemilla, derived from the unpollinated female plant, not all growers do so. And, the observations of the Commission completely ignore the fact that a marijuana plant is a renewable resource—the seeds from one plant can be used to grow several more plants. It is unrealistic, therefore, to treat one plant as representing only that amount of marijuana it can produce itself, and to require courts to assume all marijuana growers standing before them are incapable of producing more than 100 grams of marijuana per plant.

Fortunately, Congress was more realistic in establishing its mandatory minimum sentences. And, for cases involving 100 or more plants, those mandatory minimums trump the Sentencing Guidelines. The result, however, is still a boon to commercial marijuana growers who are informed enough to keep the number of plants in their operations under 100, or under 1000. That is because the interaction between the lenient Sentencing Guidelines and the stricter mandatory minimums produces a stair step effect on sentences at the 100 and 1000 plant marks. . . .

Without those mandatory minimum sentences, the Commission's view that marijuana plants should only be treated as the equivalent of 100 grams of marijuana would be controlling, which marijuana growers would doubtless applaud. Only because of the mandatory minimums does the more sensible view of Congress that each marijuana plant should be treated as the equivalent of one kilogram of marijuana impact growing operations involving 100 or more plants. Ultimately, whether the effect of those mandatory minimum sentences is good or bad depends upon how seriously one views marijuana use. If a person believes a sentence of five years is too harsh for growing 100 marijuana plants conservatively capable of producing between $26,400 to $120,000 worth of marijuana, or distributing 220 pounds of marijuana worth at least $264,000, the mandatory minimum sentences for marijuana should be abolished. If, however, a five year sentence for such crimes seems reasonable, or even lenient, the mandatory minimums should be retained, and perhaps toughened.

There is no doubt about on which side of that question the marijuana growers, dealers, users, and their supporters stand. There is also little room to doubt on which side those who take marijuana crimes seriously should stand.

"The central weakness of mandatory minimum sentences is that they substitute rigid rules for the judgment of judge and jury."

Mandatory Minimum Sentences Are Ineffective and Unfair

Dirk Chase Eldredge

In the following viewpoint, Dirk Chase Eldredge asserts that mandatory minimum sentences for drug possession have failed to reduce drug use and are an affront to judicial discretion. He argues that these laws have prevented judges from determining sentences based on the age and previous criminal record of defendants. As a result, Eldredge contends, the American legal system treats murderers and other criminals more leniently than people who have been convicted of growing or possessing marijuana. Eldredge is the author of *Ending the War on Drugs: A Solution for America*, the source of the following viewpoint.

As you read, consider the following questions:

1. By 1993, how many states had passed mandatory minimum sentencing laws?
2. Why does Eldredge claim that mandatory minimum sentences lead to "grotesque inconsistencies"?
3. According to the author, how did fifty senior federal judges respond to mandatory sentencing laws?

Dirk Chase Eldredge, *Ending the War on Drugs: A Solution for America.* Bridgehampton, NY: Bridge Works Publishing, 1998. Copyright © 1998 by Dirk Chase Eldredge. Reproduced by permission.

The Sentencing Guidelines, authorized by Congress as part of the 1984 Comprehensive Crime Control Act and the 1986 federal Mandatory Minimum Sentences System both affect a judge's discretion in sentencing convicted drug criminals.

The Origins of Mandatory Minimums

The sentencing guidelines established procedures to assist federal judges to maintain consistency in sentences from one court to the other. Armed robbery by a first-time offender with a certain amount of money involved and no bodily harm to the victim should result in the same sentence in Oklahoma as it does in Ohio, a commonsense proposition generally supported by the nation's judges. By 1993, the guidelines had been amended some 500 times but were still widely considered to help formulate more consistent and rational sentences. Guidelines can be exceeded or reduced with written justification by the judge. More than half the states have established similar procedures for state courts, and more will follow.

The story of mandatory minimum sentences is not so positive. In the ebb and flow of the war on drugs, when a surge of drug use, real or imagined, occurs, a cry goes up for a "solution." Political leaders responding to pressure from their constituents churn out more public policy to stamp out the scourge of drugs. But because these policies have an impossible objective—to eliminate illicit drug use—they are doomed to failure. Yet 46 states had passed some kind of mandatory minimum sentencing law by 1993.

When Nelson Rockefeller was governor of New York, heroin was the problem drug of the day. In 1973, in his zeal to clamp down on its burgeoning use in New York, the governor ramrodded legislation known as the Rockefeller Laws through the state legislature in Albany. A study of the efficacy of the Rockefeller Laws was commissioned by the Association of the Bar of the City of New York in 1976. It found "no evidence of a sustained reduction in heroin use after 1973" and noted that "the pattern of stable heroin use in New York City between 1973 and mid-1976 was not appreciably different from the average pattern in other East Coast cities."

Weak and Inconsistent Laws

The central weakness of mandatory minimum sentences is that they substitute rigid rules for the judgment of judge and jury. Lawrence V. Cipollone, Jr., now serving 15 years to life in New York's Downstate Correctional Facility, was arrested for selling 2.34 ounces of cocaine to an undercover officer. He points out that "Amy Fisher will be out in four years and ten months for shooting that woman in the head, and Robert Chambers got five years for the Central Park strangling." If Mr. Cipollone had been in possession of .35 of an ounce less, his sentence under the mandatory sentencing laws would have been three years. This misguided legislation also leads to the substitution by drug dealers of juveniles too young to

Herblock. © 1999 by *The Washington Post*. Reprinted with permission.

come under the jurisdiction of the sentencing laws as carriers and sellers of drugs. So large a number of arrests of minors in New York occurred that police had to quit arresting them for this offense temporarily, because the juvenile division of the criminal justice system was unable to handle the caseload.

Grotesque inconsistencies also result. Under federal law, possession of either 100 marijuana plants or 100 grams of heroin carry identical mandatory minimum sentences of 5 to 40 years without parole. In America's prisons today, there are more than 30 people serving life sentences for the crime of growing marijuana. Contrast that with an American convicted of murder who spends, on average, less than nine years in prison.

Federal Judge Alan H. Nevas of Connecticut became enormously frustrated when mandatory minimum sentencing usurped his judicial prerogatives in the case of a 20-year-old first-time offender, Keith Edwards. The transcript of the sentencing hearing reveals his outrage:

> *I have been sitting now as a judge for almost seven years. And in my view, I think the sentence which I am being forced to impose on you is one of the unfairest sentences that I have ever had to impose. Now, I don't excuse your conduct, obviously. You knew what you were doing. You were out there selling crack. You were making money, and you deserve to be punished, and you deserve to go to jail. But ten years at your age is just absolutely outrageous, as far as I'm concerned. And I resent the fact that the Congress has forced me, and put me in a position where I have to send a young man like you to jail for ten years for a crime that doesn't deserve more than three or four.*

In a similar situation, Judge J. Spencer Letts of the Central District of California was faced with a case involving 27-year-old Johnny Patillo, who had no prior criminal record, a college education and a steady job. Temporarily financially strapped, Patillo succumbed to the temptation of making a fast $500 by mailing a package, which he admitted knowing contained drugs, for a neighbor. Patillo, a basic drug "mule," was unaware of the amount or type of drug in the package: Both of these factors determined the calculation of his mandatory sentence. For his indiscretion Patillo received the mandatory minimum sentence of 10 years in prison. Like Judge Nevas in Connecticut, Judge Letts expressed his outrage:

The minimum ten-year sentence to be served by defendant was determined by Congress before he ever committed a criminal act. Congress decided to hit the problem of drugs with a sledgehammer, making no allowance for the circumstances of any particular case. Under this sledgehammer approach, it can make no difference whether defendant actually owned the drugs with which he was caught . . . It can make no difference whether he is a lifetime criminal or a first-time offender. Indeed, under this sledgehammer approach, it could make no difference if the day before making this one slip in an otherwise unblemished life, defendant had rescued 15 children from a burning building, or had won the Congressional Medal of Honor while defending his country.

A Violation of Civil Liberties

Twenty-plus years have shown that although mandatory minimum sentencing may have been well intentioned, it's also ineffective, unfair, and an insult to civil liberties. Arrests for drug law violations since the 1986 date of the federal mandatory minimum sentencing law have increased from 824,000 to over 1,500,000 in 1996. As a result, not only has a great hue and cry gone up from civil libertarians but the judicial establishment itself has emphatically said, "Enough!" The most effective statement by the judiciary came from a group of 50 of the 680 senior federal judges who announced, to the consternation of many politicians and other drug warriors, that they would no longer take drug cases because of the wrongs done by mandatory sentencing laws. This was immediately met by demands from some politicians that the judges either recant or resign. With judicial aplomb, they pointed out that as senior judges they were guided by "United States Code, Title 28, Section 294 (b), which states that a senior judge may perform such judicial duties as he is willing and able to undertake." In spite of this and other opposition, mandatory minimum drug sentences continue to exist.

"[Drug courts] are a powerful tool for addressing the criminal behavior of people who commit disproportionately large numbers of crimes."

Drug Courts Are a Promising Solution to the Drug Problem

Richard S. Gebelein

In the following viewpoint, Richard S. Gebelein argues that drug courts, which seek to rehabilitate criminals with drug arrest records through a combination of treatment, testing, and judicial supervision, have helped reduce recidivism rates. He asserts that these courts are more effective than traditional approaches such as voluntary treatment because drug courts combine treatment with specific deterrence, judicial interaction, and continuing education and monitoring. However, Gebelein cautions that while drug courts have been successful, as more varied criminals are entered into such programs, success rates are likely to fall and a backlash against drug courts could occur. Gebelein is an associate judge in the Superior Court of Delaware and the founder of Delaware's Statewide Drug Court.

As you read, consider the following questions:
1. How many drug courts had been established by the end of 1999, as stated by the author?
2. According to Gebelein, how many participants in Delaware's drug courts had their charges dismissed?
3. In what other area might the drug court approach be useful, in the author's opinion?

Richard S. Gebelein, "The Rebirth of Rehabilitation: Promise and Perils of Drug Courts," *Sentencing & Corrections: Issues for the 21st Century*, May 2000. Copyright © 2000 by Richard S. Gebelein. Reproduced by permission.

D rug cases began to escalate dramatically in the 1980s. Petty drug offenders were recycling through the justice system at an alarming rate. Delaware's situation was typical. Overwhelmed with drug cases, the State's courts sought ways to manage case flow and solve the "revolving door" problem. Courts everywhere also sought sentencing alternatives for addicted offenders.

The situation brought to the fore questions about the link of substance abuse to crime. About this time, research was shedding better light on the issue. A study conducted in 1987 revealed that a large proportion of arrestees in several major urban areas tested positive for illegal substances. When the Delaware drug court was in the design stage, a study of the State's prisoners revealed that 80 percent needed substance abuse treatment. Researchers were also finding that when addicted offenders used drugs, they were among the most active perpetrators of other crimes.

At the same time, it was becoming established that if treatment reduced drug use by criminally involved addicts, it would also reduce their tendency to commit crime. Research was also proving that compelled treatment was as effective as voluntary treatment. Delaware would find, and other research would confirm, that in-prison treatment based on the therapeutic community (TC) model dramatically affects drug use and recidivism.

The Emergence of Drug Courts

All these factors converged to create a climate conducive to the growth of drug courts. When the National Association of Drug Court Professionals (NADCP) was established in 1994, the drug court judges who founded it numbered fewer than 15. Only 5 years later, the NADCP's annual training meeting drew 3,000 participants. About 10 years after Miami created what was arguably the first drug court, there were drug courts in almost every State and the District of Columbia. The expansion to more than 400 by the end of 1999 is evidence of the movement's popularity.

The movement gained wide acceptance for many of the reasons rehabilitation did in the 1950s. It offered hope of solving a grave problem. It is innovative, leveraging the court's power to compel drug-involved offenders to use a method that works—treatment. Its advantage over "plain old" rehabilitation is the focus on one problem (addiction) that is causally related to crime committed by one group of offenders (addicts). Treatment is reinforced with a healthy dose of specific deterrence as a motivation to achieve a specific result—abstinence. Federal legislation provided an added impetus, as the 1994 Crime Act provided funding to establish or expand drug courts.

The nature, structure, and jurisdiction of drug courts vary widely. Given the many variations, it became important to achieve consensus on what is a "true" drug court. The NADCP and the U.S. Department of Justice identified the following key elements:

- Integration of substance abuse treatment with justice system case processing.
- Use of a nonadversarial approach, in which prosecution and defense promote public safety while protecting the right of the accused to due process.
- Early identification and prompt placement of eligible participants.
- Access to a continuum of treatment, rehabilitation, and related services.
- Frequent testing for alcohol and illicit drugs.
- A coordinated strategy among judge, prosecution, defense, and treatment providers to govern offender compliance.
- Ongoing judicial interaction with each participant.
- Monitoring and evaluation to measure achievement of program goals and gauge effectiveness.
- Continuing interdisciplinary education to promote effective planning, implementation, and operation.
- Partnerships with public agencies and community-based organizations to generate local support and enhance drug court effectiveness.

Most drug courts attempt to integrate these components. One reason is that Federal funding is contingent on a plan that incorporates them all.

In general, the offender enters the program through a plea, conditional plea, contract with the court, or similar mechanism. The offender is assigned to a treatment program and told when to report to court. Court appearances can be as frequent as several times a week or can be once a month or less often. Urinalysis is frequent and usually on a random basis. Urinalysis positives or missed treatments or court appointments result in immediate sanctions. In Delaware's diversionary court, requirements include 4 months of total abstinence in addition to holding a steady job, successfully completing treatment, earning a general equivalency diploma if applicable, participating in 12-step meetings, developing a support network, and maintaining a stable residence.

The Role of Judges

The most original feature of drug court is the judge's active participation in the patient's treatment, which brings to bear his considerable symbolic authority. The judge's involvement refines drug court's coercive edge through the instantaneous graduated punishments he can mete out. Prior to the emergence of drug courts, a judge who recommended drug treatment as a condition of sentencing would refer the offender to a treatment program and then see him once or twice again, if ever. Today, during regularly scheduled courtroom hearings, the judge holds the defendant publicly accountable for his progress. Technically, a mere magistrate could do the judge's work, but the powerful effect of the judicial black robe on the offender "can't be underestimated," according to Jeffrey Tauber, a former judge who presided over Oakland's drug court and who now serves as president of the National Association of Drug Court Professionals. "It shows defendants that we take this process seriously," he says.

Sally Satel, *City Journal*, Summer 1998.

The first drug courts dealt primarily with minor drug offenses, with offenders placed on a diversionary or quasi-diversionary track. Newer designs include postadjudicative drug courts (those in which the offender is sentenced to drug court after conviction), juvenile drug courts, and family drug courts. In the model most commonly used today, the population of substance-abusing offenders is wider and more varied than that of the first drug courts. Drug courts funded by the 1994 Crime Act may process only nonviolent offenders, but many drug courts that are wholly State funded or locally funded accept some violent offenders.

Delaware's drug courts in many respects typify drug courts in general. They began with an effort to solve the problem of drugs and crime. The State's Drug Involved Offender Coordination Committee, organized in 1991 to weigh proposed solutions, discovered flaws in the State's approach to offender substance abuse. Many court orders referring defendants to treatment were ignored by corrections officials. Related problems came to light. Offenders were more likely than non-court-referred participants to be discharged from treatment programs. Jail- or prison-based treatment was limited; there was no coordination between treatment in jail and the community; and treatment was inefficiently delivered and inadequate in relation to the need.

A treatment continuum did not exist. To create one, the Treatment Access Committee (TAC) was established and charged with ensuring that substance-abusing offenders did not "fall through the cracks."

Targeted Groups

Delaware's potential treatment population was so large that only two groups could be targeted. Younger offenders, who are less criminally involved and who can possibly be diverted from a life of crime, were selected as one group.

The diversion track calls for a modest "investment" of 6 months to a year in drug court, with outpatient treatment and frequent urine tests. These offenders are not under sentence, so they are not supervised by probation. This saves resources, which can be used to supervise more serious offenders. However, offenders on this track are more accountable than those on regular probation. If the offender cannot stay drug free or otherwise fails, diversion is terminated, a trial is held, and, if it results in conviction, the usual sentence is probation with compelled treatment. If all conditions are met, the offender graduates and the charge is dismissed.

Offenders in jail or prison because of violating probation were another group identified as needing substantial investment of treatment resources. TAC felt that a drug court model could work with them, although outpatient treatment without probation supervision was unlikely to work with many. This group of more serious offenders consists largely of people convicted of 6 to 10 felonies and addicted for 12 to 20 years. The probation revocation model is for offenders charged with a new crime. The prosecutor offers to resolve the new offense and the probation violation simultaneously, through a plea and an "addiction sentence" that always includes drug court–supervised treatment. If the defendant accepts the offer, he or she is immediately sentenced on both counts. If the defendant is sentenced to jail or prison, he or she enters a treatment program in the correctional facility. Successful completion means the remaining prison time is suspended and replaced with supervision and treatment in the community. The addiction sentence allows the court to require this treatment continuum through the in-prison "Key" program, followed by work release and continued treatment in the "Crest" program and aftercare in the community. In effect, the model provides for indeterminate sentencing—tailored to the offender, with the goal of rehabilitation—in a truth-in-sentencing State.

All addiction sentences require frequent court appearances, and the assignment of a Treatment Alternatives to Street Crime (TASC) case manager, to ensure continuum of treatment in the transition from jail to halfway house to community. Failure in this track usually results in a prison sentence with an order to participate in a long-term therapeutic community while incarcerated, followed again by treatment in the community, with reentry monitored by the drug court.

Promising Results

Scientifically based evaluations of Delaware's drug courts are not completed, but initial studies are encouraging. The figures on numbers of diversion track graduates are a rough estimate: By the end of 1999, charges were dismissed for 2,670 people—about half of those who entered the program. Case studies demonstrate that the lives of people once considered total criminal justice failures have been saved. The widespread belief among judges, prosecutors, defense attorneys, and others that the Delaware drug courts are working and turning lives around cannot easily be discounted.

Treatment providers indicated 18 months into the program that their drug court clients are more likely to complete treatment than are their other clients, and that they stay in treatment longer. Preliminary evaluation results suggest that Delaware drug court graduates reoffend less often than other sentenced offenders and, when they do, their crimes are on average far less serious. Studies of drug courts in other jurisdictions offer similarly encouraging findings. The past 3 years' experience in Delaware indicates that offenders adjudicated through the probation revocation track spend less time in prison than do other offenders sentenced for similar crimes. This is because drug court offenders can earn early release by completing treatment.

Drug courts will not solve the drug problem or eliminate crime in Delaware or anywhere else. But if they offer a comprehensive treatment continuum, solid case management, and meaningful immediate sanctions, they can have a major effect on public safety. They are a powerful tool for addressing the criminal behavior of people who commit disproportionately large numbers of crimes. . . .

The Perils of Drug Courts

The drug court movement is currently riding a wave of success. Initial evaluations are favorable. New courts are being established everywhere. The movement is supported by both major political parties and the news media. Even more important, it has captured the imagination of the public. Ironically, success is perhaps the biggest peril drug courts face.

Success with a narrowly defined offender population does not translate into a universal solution to drug crime.

As the results of more sophisticated evaluations become available, preliminary success rates will not be sustained. As less tractable groups participate, rates of compliance and graduation will decline and recidivism will rise. Support may fade as success appears to diminish. The movement cannot afford to claim too much and so must define success realistically.

Differences in treatment options and in groups that participate will affect outcomes. Some drug courts, such as

186

Delaware's probation revocation track, include a full spectrum of treatment options. Others, such as Delaware's diversion track, rely primarily on outpatient treatment, drug education, and urine tests. Success is likely to vary with the treatment available.

In Delaware's probation revocation track, the participants are far more involved with drugs and other crime than those on the diversion track, who are younger, are less severely addicted, and have less extensive criminal histories. Different success rates can be expected from the different populations.

In identifying target populations, drug courts need to be sensitive to class and race bias, real or apparent. Unless care is taken, diversion courts may tend disproportionately to work with white and middle-class substance abusers. In Delaware, the client demographics of the diversion and probation revocation tracks were at first virtual opposites. Participants in the latter were disproportionately minority group members from disadvantaged backgrounds; those in the former were more likely to be white and middle class. Delaware has aggressively addressed this imbalance.

Differences in populations and treatments can lead to the same problems that came to light in research on boot camps. Initially, boot camps were highly popular (perhaps for all the wrong reasons). They proliferated quickly, and claims of success abounded. However, evaluations generally revealed that boot camps do little to reduce recidivism. As a result, funding eroded, fewer resources were allocated, and support all but evaporated. The same fate could befall drug courts if evaluations of individual courts that offer incomplete treatment or no real treatment at all reveal low success rates. . . .

Unrealistic Expectations

Americans want quick, decisive solutions. This is evident in the very terminology used for this national propensity: We wage a "War on Drugs." Yet as General Barry McCaffrey, [former] head of the Office of National Drug Control Policy, has noted, the problem cannot be solved this way. War requires concentrated maximum force at a critical point. For the drug problem, there is no silver bullet, nor is there a single program, model, or method that will eliminate either addiction or crime.

Because drug courts are effective in helping address one correlate of crime, they may also serve as a model to help address others. Research may reveal whether this expectation is realistic by demonstrating why drug courts work and whether similar principles are likely to work for groups other than drug-involved offenders. Delaware's proposed reentry court for nonaddicted offenders is an example of the extension of the model.

Judges tend to deal more often with failure than success. Many drug court judges, enthusiastic about their perceived successes, may yield to the temptation to claim they have the key to winning the war on drugs and criminal behavior. That claim will surely fail to be sustained. Instances of failure of the drug court method will become more widely reported. The movement's claims will be tested against results. If the claims of judges and others are unreasonably optimistic and not based in reality, backlash is inevitable.

Expanding the Drug Court Model

The drug court movement focused initially on adult drug offenders who had histories of nonviolent offenses. Depending on the site, the movement now encompasses offenders convicted of several felonies, many of whom have criminal histories that qualify them for habitual offender status. The movement also extends to specialty courts dedicated to juvenile offending, domestic violence, and family issues and has fostered establishment of treatment courts for DUI cases.

There are other areas where the drug court approach may be useful. An example is "therapeutic jurisprudence," a new, problem-solving orientation adopted by some judges, courts, and court systems. Participants in the drug court movement believe that success is due in large part to direct judicial involvement with offenders, provided on a regular basis. It is likely that judges who have been successful with the approach will want to apply it to other areas.

In expanding the drug court model to clients other than drug users, care must be taken until more is known about why the process works and with what types of offenders it might be effective. That means first designing pilot programs, implementing them, and evaluating them. Drug courts hold great promise as a tool to prevent crime in the long term. For that to become reality, every effort must be taken to avoid the many perils that could make the movement just another failed criminal justice fad.

> *"Drug courts not only don't accomplish their goals but they may be widening the criminal justice net."*

Drug Courts Have Not Reduced the Drug Problem

Melissa Hostetler

Drug courts are an approach to punishment and rehabilitation that combines judicial discretion with sanctions, treatments, and drug testing. Melissa Hostetler reports in the following viewpoint that these courts are not as successful as their advocates claim. She claims that instead of reducing drug possession offenses, drug courts have resulted in an increase in arrests. In addition, Hostetler explains, drug courts discourage states from funding voluntary treatment and give too much power to judges, who often are not qualified to determine the proper course of treatment for drug offenders. Hostetler is a journalist and cofounder of Frictionmagazine.com.

As you read, consider the following questions:

1. By how much did drug filings in Denver increase in the first two years of its drug court program, according to the author?
2. According to Hostetler, why have drug courts not saved money?
3. Why does Dr. John McCarthy criticize the role of judges in drug courts?

Melissa Hostetler, "Rethinking Drug Courts," *Clamor*, March/April 2002. Copyright © 2002 by Melissa Hostetler. Reproduced by permission.

W elcome to the San Francisco County drug court, just one of nearly a thousand courts in the country and one of more than a hundred in California alone offering drug treatment over incarceration. The court begins to come alive as the defendants—or clients as drug court professionals like to call them—arrive and speak in hushed tones with their counselors and attorneys.

In the hall, a counselor hugs a client twice her size and encourages him to stay with the treatment program. The client is later sent to jail on Judge Julie Tang's order for testing positive for drugs. Though this weekend-long prison stay is only considered a sanction, this client may very well end up in jail long-term.

A female clad in an orange jumper sits and watches as a half dozen soon to be ex-clients tell their story of how treatment and a second chance has changed their lives. As a new drug court recruit, she hears about their new jobs, new lives, and a new outlook on staying sober. She decides drug court is for her—the freedom of a probation-style life, the allure of having all charges dropped upon completion of the program, and the hope of finally being rid of the drug addiction disease seem all too convincing.

Looking More Closely at Drug Courts

And though the argument for treatment-based drug courts seems convincing—the media are sold on the idea of treatment over prison, and the drug court movement is picking up steam as politicians who strive to be tough on crime and compassionate in one swoop are singing its praises—there are many who are starting to question whether or not the drug court movement is the panacea of good will everyone says it is.

Since the first treatment-based program was founded in Miami, Florida, [in the early 1990s,] the drug court epidemic has spread to nearly every state, adding up to more than 800 drug courts nationwide either operating or in the planning stages. US federal funding for the program now totals more than $80 million since 1995 in a political phenomenon that is getting support from all sides. Actor Martin Sheen, former Drug Czar Barry McCaffrey, and [former] Attorney General Janet Reno (who helped found the Florida drug court when she was Florida Attorney General) have lined up behind the program.

They call them the elixir to cure prison overcrowding, the cycling of drug offenders in and out of the criminal justice system, and the skyrocketing price-tag of the US prison system. In a closer look though, many have found that drug courts not only don't accomplish their goals but they may be widening the criminal justice net, increasing costs to the system, taking treatment slots away from voluntary, community-based programs, and blurring the traditional roles of judges, prosecutors, and defense attorneys.

"Drug courts are just the latest Band-Aid we have tried to apply over the deep wound of our schizophrenia about drugs," says Denver, Colorado, Judge Morris B. Hoffman in a *North Carolina Law* review article that is one of the few critical pieces on drug courts. "Drug courts themselves have become a kind of institutional narcotic upon which the entire criminal justice system is becoming increasingly dependent."

Though they are designed to relieve the criminal justice system of some of its burden—one in four American prisoners is incarcerated for a non-violent drug offense—drug courts may actually be increasing the number of people brought into the system and thus also negating most of their expected savings.

"What we've started to see happening is people who previously would have essentially not been arrested at all or given a short term of probation or a fine wound up getting arrested," says Katherine Huffman of the Lindesmith Center for Drug Policy Foundation.

Arrests Have Increased

In Denver, drug filings tripled just two years into the drug court program. Not only had the number tripled, but the percentage of drug filings went from 30 percent of all filings to 52 percent in that same period.

California, home to more than 100 drug courts, also saw drug arrests for possession only offenses increase from 40 percent of all drug arrests to 53 percent in the past ten years. It is not clear though what effect if any drug courts have made directly.

"All we know is that drug courts have not resulted in fewer people sentenced to prison for drug possession offenses in California," says Dan Macalair of the Justice Policy Institute. "In fact, the evidence is just the opposite." The increased arrests, says Jeff Tauber, president of the National Association of Drug Court Professionals, is that the justice system has chosen to start dealing with those previously ignored. By bringing offenders into the system early on, drug courts can avoid repeated offenses, he says.

A survey suggests, though, that law enforcement see drug courts as a solution to America's drug problems. Two-thirds of the 300 police chiefs polled in a survey do not want to cut federal drug court funding, and 60 percent claim drug courts are more effective than prison or jail time.

"The very presence of the drug court has caused police to make arrests in, and prosecutors to file, the kinds of ten- and twenty-dollar hand-to-hand drug cases that the system simply would not have bothered with before, certainly not as felonies," says Judge Hoffman.

Costly and Ineffective

With the increased number of drug offenders coming into the criminal justice system, the cost savings promised by drug courts are largely non-existent. According to the Vera Institute of Justice, many cost-savings analyses fail to account for common drug court practices that ultimately erode savings—detaining offenders for detoxification and punishing non-complaint participants with jail time. When interim jail stays are counted, drug court participants could spend more time in jail than if they had simply been sentenced. The Vera Institute also found evidence to suggest that participants who fail in drug court may be sentenced more harshly than those never entering a drug court.

The problem though with determining whether or not drug courts are actually working is in the research itself.

For example, drug courts claim to reduce the cycle of drug offenders coming in and out of the prison system. The Department of Justice's Drug Courts Program Office claims a reduction in recidivism between five and 28 percent, but not all studies show these results. An Arizona drug court study found no difference in recidivism between those in standard probation and those in drug court. Another evaluation of 21 drug courts found that five could not claim they reduced recidivism. The problem says Judge Hoffman is the method of evaluation. Drug court professionals who have a vested interest in continuing the program are often the ones doing the drug court impact studies, resulting in what is little more than a morale booster for drug court professionals.

The very nature of localized drug courts allows for survey results that cannot be compared. Without a comprehensive data source, there is no telling how well the drug court program is actually working, says Macalair. Not to mention, he adds, the surveys themselves do not seem to be asking the right questions—for example, true cost analyses of drug court treatment programs have seldom been done.

Tauber says the results are not solely in speculated recidivism improvements. Retention, he says, is the defining factor of how well the program is working, citing that drug courts keep people in treatment longer making it more likely they will stick to their new lifestyle.

Drug Courts Versus Treatment

But on top of these woes are the concerns for the larger picture of drug treatment in America.

Most who question the drug court strategy prefer treatment to incarceration, but would rather see resources put into voluntary treatment and court-mandated treatment. But instead of creating new slots to answer the call of the thousands waiting for treatment, drug courts are absorbing some of these treatment slots, says Graham Boyd, director of the ACLU Drug Litigation Project.

Drug courts have flourished largely because of the enormous political support given them. But there is no such will for adding more community-based treatment, leaving the system skewed in favor of the criminal justice system at the cost of voluntary treatment, says Daniel Abrahamson, director of legal affairs for the Lindesmith Center.

It's logical to want to treat everyone, Tauber says, but the motivation and consequences of drug court are much stronger

194

and tangible for addicts to complete the program and get off drugs than if they entered treatment on their own. In fact, Tauber says drug courts provide better results than voluntary treatment because they tend to keep addicts in treatment longer.

Drug Courts and Rearrests

James L. Nolan Jr. discusses the 1993 American Bar Association study of drug courts in his book *The Therapeutic State*. The study found that among offenders who were sent to the Drug Court, 20% were rearrested for a drug offense and 32% were rearrested for any felony offense within one year of the sampled arrest. Among pre–Drug Court defendants, 23% were rearrested for a narcotics offense and 33% for any felony offense within one year. He further notes, "Again, they found little difference between the samples. Drug offenders sent through the Drug Court were rearrested, on average, 324 days after their first court appearance, whereas drug offenders sentenced prior to the Drug Court were rearrested, on average, 319 days after their first court appearance."

Common Sense for Drug Policy, *Factbook: Drug Courts and Treatment as an Alternative to Incarceration*, 2002.

But even if drug courts are working, their essential nature runs contrary to the traditional roles of the justice system. That, say critics, is not only bad for drug court defendants but for the public as well.

Too Much Judicial Discretion

This non-adversarial nature found in drug courts—where the judge, the prosecutor, and the defense attorney are all working toward the uniform goal keeping the defendant in treatment—is precisely why drug courts work, say drug court professionals. Drug court judges are able to exercise a fair amount of discretion, thus making the system more tailored for each individual. The drug court system though allows judges to become social workers and pseudo-doctors, and critics say this is not the type of discretion that the criminal justice system needs or deserves. The judicial branch, they say, is not the arena for handling what is essentially a public policy issue.

"The real problem with the drug courts is that the judges don't know what treatment is," says Dr. John McCarthy, a psychiatrist and addiction medicine specialist at the Bi-Valley Medical Clinic in Sacramento. Judges aren't doctors, he says, and the drug court structure makes "every judge his own king."

Though in some jurisdictions treatment professionals are in the court to directly advise a judge on what to do, the judge ultimately gets to make the final decisions.

"I cannot imagine a more dangerous branch than an unrestrained judiciary full of amateur psychiatrists poised to 'do good' rather than to apply the law," says Judge Hoffman.

Noble but Problematic

The drug court method, in fact, is just the first sample of what may come if the problem-solving court model spreads to the arenas of domestic violence, mental health, and prostitution as many like Tauber hope it will. To function, these courts will need these non-traditional roles and judges willing to institute them, says San Francisco Superior Court Judge Julie Tang.

"In other courts, the outcome is punishment and rehabilitation if necessary," she says. "In our case it's rehabilitation as the goal and purpose of the court. You need to have a different structure to produce outcomes."

Though the idea may be a noble and humane one—helping people and keeping them out of prison—critics say it is wrong to treat these problems as diseases and then punish offenders in a system where no one is working for the offenders themselves. And in a system that is being exported across borders—Canada's federal government has plans to set up drug courts in very major city by 2004—this, critics say, could end in a strange downward spiral where the judicial system serves the welfare state and no one serves the law or the people.

Periodical Bibliography

The following articles have been selected to supplement the diverse views presented in this chapter.

Mary H. Cooper	"Drug-Policy Debate," *CQ Researcher*, July 28, 2000.
John J. DiIulio Jr.	"Against Mandatory Minimums," *National Review*, May 17, 1999.
Dirk Chase Eldredge and Bill McCollum	"Symposium: Would Legalizing Drugs Serve America's National Interest?" *Insight on the News*, September 14, 1998.
Jim Gray, interviewed by *Drug Policy Letter*	"Jim Gray on *Control v. Prohibition*," *Drug Policy Letter*, Spring 1998.
Issues and Controversies on File	"Drug Courts," February 15, 2002.
Gary E. Johnson, interviewed by Michael W. Lynch	"America's Most Dangerous Politician," *Reason*, January 2001.
Eduard Lintner	"Germany: A Strict Approach," *World & I*, October 1998.
Michael Massing	"New Ideas for Ending the War on Drugs," *Nation*, September 20, 1999.
Deroy Murdock and Don Feder	"Symposium: Pros and Cons of Marijuana Legalization," *Insight on the News*, October 1, 2001.
Progressive	"A Sane Drug Policy," October 1999.
Charles B. Rangel	"Why Drug Legalization Should Be Opposed," *Criminal Justice Ethics*, Summer/Fall 1998.
William Ratliff	"Colombia's Drug War Must Be Won in the U.S.," *Los Angeles Times*, February 11, 2001.
Helen Redmond	"The War on Drugs: Myth and Reality," *International Socialist Review*, December 2000/January 2001.
Bill Ritter	"Fighting the Real War on Drugs," *World & I*, February 2000.
Sally Satel	"Do Drug Courts Really Work?" *City Journal*, Summer 1998.
Wall Street Journal	"Drive-Thru Highs," May 9, 2001.

For Further Discussion

Chapter 1

1. Tom Shales and Mike Males argue that the media exaggerate the problem of chemical dependency. Have media reports affected your views on drugs? Explain.

2. Robert A. Levy asserts that tobacco is a relatively less damaging substance than alcohol or drugs. One reason he gives for this argument is that tobacco-related deaths tend to come later in life. What are your views on this contention? Do you agree with the rest of his comparison between tobacco and other substances? Explain your answer.

3. After reading the viewpoints by Michelle Meadows and Tom Shales, what do you think will be the future of OxyContin? Explain your answer.

Chapter 2

1. Alan Leshner and Sally Satel disagree on whether addiction can be considered a brain disease. Whose argument do you find more convincing and why?

2. In his viewpoint, Ernest P. Noble writes that during most of the twentieth century, addiction was viewed as a personal flaw. Do you believe that is true today? Why or why not?

3. After reading the viewpoints by Susan M. Gordon and the Office of National Drug Control Policy and Substance Abuse and Mental Health Services Administration, which factors do you believe play the greatest role in determining teenage drug abuse? Explain your answer.

Chapter 3

1. Peter Beilenson asserts that needle-exchange programs reduce the spread of the AIDS virus and do not encourage drug use. Joe Loconte contends that studies claiming to prove the effectiveness of these programs are flawed. After reading their viewpoints, do you believe that the scientific evidence supports the use of needle-exchange programs, or are these programs an ineffective panacea? Explain your answers.

2. After reading the viewpoints by Robert H. Hood and Mary Faith Marshall, what do you believe should take precedence: the privacy rights of pregnant women or the health of their fetuses? In addition, do you believe drug tests of pregnant women are discriminatory? Explain your answer, drawing from the viewpoints and any other relevant material.

3. Which of the treatments presented in this chapter do you believe is most effective at treating chemical dependency? What other treatments do you think would be useful and why?

Chapter 4

1. The first four viewpoints in this chapter evaluate the success of the war on drugs and question whether some illegal drugs should be decriminalized. Based on your reading of these viewpoints, do you think U.S. policy on drug use should be changed? Explain.

2. After reading the viewpoints by David Risley and Dirk Chase Eldredge, do you believe mandatory minimum sentences help reduce the sale and possession of drugs? If yes, do you think such sentences should be toughened? If no, what do you believe are the main problems with mandatory minimums? Explain your answers.

3. Melissa Hostetler claims that one of the flaws of drug courts is that they give too much power to judges. Do you believe that this concern is justified? Why or why not?

Organizations to Contact

The editors have compiled the following list of organizations concerned with issues debated in this book. The descriptions are derived from materials provided by the organizations. All have publications or information available for interested readers. The list was compiled on the date of publication of the present volume; the information provided here may change. Be aware that many organizations take several weeks or longer to respond to inquiries, so allow as much time as possible.

Alcoholics Anonymous (AA)
Grand Central Station, PO Box 459, New York, NY 10163
(212) 870-3400 • fax: (212) 870-3003
website: www.aa.org

Alcoholics Anonymous is a worldwide fellowship of sober alcoholics, whose recovery is based on twelve steps. AA's primary purpose is to carry the AA message to the alcoholic who still suffers. Its publications include the book *Alcoholics Anonymous* (more commonly known as the Big Book) and the pamphlets *A Brief Guide to Alcoholics Anonymous, Young People and AA*, and *AA Traditions—How It Developed*.

Canadian Centre on Substance Abuse (CCSA)
75 Albert St., Suite 300, Ottawa, ON K1P 5E7 Canada
(613) 235-4048 • fax: (613) 235-8101
e-mail: info@ccsa.ca • website: www.ccsa.ca

Established in 1988 by an act of Parliament, the CCSA works to minimize the harm associated with the use of alcohol, tobacco, and other drugs by sponsoring public debates on this issue. It disseminates information on the nature, extent, and consequences of substance abuse and supports organizations involved in substance abuse treatment, prevention, and educational programming. The center publishes the newsletter *Action News* six times a year.

The Lindesmith Center-Drug Policy Foundation (TLC-DPF)
4455 Connecticut Ave. NW, Suite B-500, Washington, DC 20008-2328
(202) 537-5005 • fax: (202) 537-3007
e-mail: information@drugpolicy.org • website: www.lindesmith.org

The Lindesmith Center-Drug Policy Foundation seeks to educate Americans and others about alternatives to current drug policies on issues including adolescent drug use, policing drug markets, and alternatives to incarceration. TLC-DPF also addresses issues of drug policy reform through a variety of projects and publishes fact sheets on topics such as needle and syringe availability and drug education.

Narcotics Anonymous (NA)
World Services Office, PO Box 9999, Van Nuys, CA 91409
(818) 773-9999 • fax: (818) 700-0700
Narcotics Anonymous, comprising more than eighteen thousand groups worldwide, is an organization of recovering drug addicts who meet regularly to help each other abstain from drugs. It publishes the monthly *NA Way Magazine* and annual conference reports.

National Center on Addiction and Substance Abuse at Columbia University (CASA)
633 3rd Ave., 19th Fl., New York, NY 10017-6706
(212) 841-5200
website: www.casacolumbia.org
CASA is a private, nonprofit organization that works to educate the public about the hazards of chemical dependency. The organization supports treatment as the best way to reduce chemical dependency. It produces publications describing the harmful effects of alcohol and drug addiction and effective ways to address the problem of substance abuse. Its reports include the "National Survey of American Attitudes on Substance Abuse VI: Teens" and "Research on Drug Courts."

National Institute on Alcohol Abuse and Alcoholism (NIAAA)
Willco Building, 6000 Executive Blvd., Bethesda, MD 20892-7003
(301) 496-4000
e-mail: niaaaweb-r@exchange.nih.gov
website: www.niaaa.nih.gov
NIAAA supports and conducts biomedical and behavioral research on the causes, consequences, treatment, and prevention of alcoholism and alcohol-related problems. The institute disseminates its findings to the public, researchers, policymakers, and health care providers. The NIAAA publishes the quarterly journal *Alcohol Research & Health*, *Alcohol Alert* bulletins, pamphlets, and reports.

Office of National Drug Control Policy (ONDCP)
Drug Policy Information Clearinghouse
PO Box 6000, Rockville, MD 20849-6000
(800) 666-3332 • fax: (301) 519-5212
e-mail: ondcp@ncjrs.org • website: www.whitehousedrugpolicy.gov
The Office of National Drug Control Policy formulates the government's national drug strategy and the president's antidrug policy and coordinates the federal agencies responsible for stopping drug trafficking. Its reports include "National Drug Control Strategy, 2002" and "Get It Straight! The Facts About Drugs."

Bibliography of Books

Rachel Green Baldino   *Welcome to Methadonia: A Social Worker's Candid Account of Life in a Methadone Clinic.* Harrisburg, PA: White Hat Communications, 2001.

Rosalyn Carson-Dewitt and Joseph W. Weiss, eds.   *Drugs, Alcohol, and Tobacco: Learning About Addictive Behavior.* New York: MacMillan Reference Books, 2003.

Andrew Cherry, Mary E. Dillon, and Douglas Rugh, eds.   *Substance Abuse: A Global View.* Westport, CT: Greenwood Press, 2002.

Rod Colvin   *Prescription Drug Addiction: The Hidden Epidemic.* Omaha, NE: Addicus Books, 2001.

Ross Coomber, ed.   *The Control of Drugs and Drug Users: Reason or Reaction?* Amsterdam: Harwood Academic, 1998.

Robert L. Dupont and Betty Ford   *The Selfish Brain: Learning from Addiction.* Washington, DC: Hazelden Information Education, 2000.

Dirk Chase Eldredge   *Ending the War on Drugs: A Solution for America.* Bridgehampton, NY: Bridge Works Publishing Company, 1998.

R. Barri Flowers   *Drugs, Alcohol and Criminality in American Society.* Jefferson, NC: McFarland & Company, 1999.

Marcus Grant and Jorge Litvak, eds.   *Drinking Patterns and Their Consequences.* Washington, DC: Taylor & Francis, 1998.

James P. Gray   *Why Our Drug Laws Have Failed and What We Can Do About It: A Judicial Indictment on the War on Drugs.* Philadelphia: Temple University Press, 2001.

Mike Gray   *Drug Crazy: How We Got into This Mess and How We Can Get Out.* New York: Random House, 1998.

Jeffrey R. Guss and Jack Drescher, eds.   *Addictions in the Gay and Lesbian Community.* Binghamton, NY: Haworth Medical Press, 2000.

Ansley Hamid   *Drugs in America: Sociology, Economics, and Politics.* Gaithersburg, MD: Aspen Publishers, 1998.

Glen Hanson, Peter Venturelli, and Annette E. Fleckenstein, eds.   *Drugs and Society.* Boston: Jones and Bartlett, 2001.

Raymond V. Haring	*Shattering Myths and Mysteries of Alcohol: Insights and Answers to Drinking, Smoking, and Drug Use.* Sacramento: Healthspan Communications, 1998.
Philip B. Heymann and William N. Brownsberger, eds.	*Drug Addiction and Drug Policy: The Struggle to Control Dependence.* Cambridge, MA: Harvard University Press, 2001.
Rachel Kranz	*Straight Talk About Smoking.* New York: Facts On File, 1999.
Jennifer Lawler	*Drug Legalization: A Pro/Con Issue.* Berkeley Heights, NJ: Enslow, 1999.
David M. MacDowell and Henry I. Spitz	*Substance Abuse: From Principles to Practice.* Philadelphia: Brunner/Mazel, 1999.
Michael Massing	*The Fix.* New York: Simon and Schuster, 1998.
Ann Marie Pagliaro and Louis A. Pagliaro	*Substance Use Among Women: A Reference and Resource Guide.* Philadelphia: Brunner/Mazel, 2000.
Stanton Peele	*The Diseasing of America: How We Allowed Recovery Zealots and the Treatment Industry to Convince Us We Are Out of Control.* San Francisco: Jossey-Bass, 1999.
Philip Robson	*Forbidden Drugs.* New York: Oxford University Press, 1999.
Jeffrey A. Schaler, ed.	*Drugs: Should We Legalize, Decriminalize, or Deregulate?* Amherst, NY: Prometheus, 1998.
Marc Allen Schuckit	*Educating Yourself About Drugs and Alcohol: A People's Primer.* New York: Plenum Trade, 1998.
Ben Sonder	*All About Heroin.* New York: Franklin Watts, 2002.
Jacob Sullum	*For Your Own Good: The Anti-Smoking Crusade and the Tyranny of Public Health.* New York: Free Press, 1998.
Patsy Westcott	*Why Do People Take Drugs?* Austin, TX: Raintree Steck-Vaughn Publishers, 2001.

Index